DATE DUE

DATE DUE	
DEC 1 1 1998	
NOV 1 7 2000	
JAN 2 6 2002	
APR 0 6 2003	
FEB 2 2 2005	

GAYLORD   PRINTED IN U.S.A.

THE MARINER'S ROLE IN COLLECTING EVIDENCE
(SECOND EDITION)

Compiled by
a Special Working Group of
the North East Branch
of
The Nautical Institute

Chairman and General Editor:
Captain Phil Anderson, BA (Hons), FNI

Editorial Consultant:
Ms. Reena Mohamedi

Individual Committee members of the Working Group and
other contributors are mentioned in the "Contents" pages
against their particular topic area.

Published by The Nautical Institute
202 Lambeth Road, London SE1 7LQ, England
Telephone: 0171 928 1351

Second edition published 1997

Typeset by Tradeset Ltd, Southall, Middlesex

Printed in England by O'Sullivan Printing Corporation, Southall, Middlesex

ISBN 1 870077 05 9

Admiralty Court

FOREWORD I

By The Honourable Mr Justice Clarke

Some time ago I was asked to contribute a few thoughts to put at the beginning of the video which has been produced to complement this book. The following occurred to me:

> *Courts depend upon evidence. Contemporary evidence is of the utmost importance. It is vital to make a note or report of any incident immediately, if possible while it is still in progress. Photographic or video evidence is of particular assistance to the judge or arbitrator in trying to establish the true facts.*

It seemed to me then that the video underlined those truths. So does this valuable book, but on a more comprehensive scale.

Casualties and incidents of one kind or another are bound to occur from time to time in the navigation and operation of ships. When they do, legal disputes are not unlikely to arise – especially in these combative times. The principal aim of the sensible cargo-owner, charterer and shipowner is of course to settle them quickly and cheaply, but fairly. If a dispute cannot be settled it may have to be determined by arbitration or litigation.

Contrary to popular belief, judges and arbitrators cannot simply invent evidence. They rely upon the oral and written statements of witnesses, but more importantly they rely upon contemporary documents which come into existence at the time of the casualty or incident. Contemporary log entries and reports made immediately are regarded as more likely to be reliable than statements made much later after discussion with, say, a marine or engineer superintendent or a solicitor, who may have suggested a party line to the witness.

It can immediately be seen that the mariner's role is of vital importance. He is, after all, the man (or woman) on the spot. It follows that a book of this kind is of inestimable value. The more contemporary material that is available the more likely it is that a dispute can be settled on satisfactory terms. It should be remembered that, even if the shipowner is liable, it will often be much more sensible, less time consuming and less expensive to settle at an early stage rather than to spend many years incurring legal fees and ultimately settling for much more, including payment of the other side's legal costs.

I am very pleased to note that this book stresses not only the importance of log books, operation records and informal notes made at the time, but also the fact that of equal or greater importance is evidence which cannot lie, such as photographs, videos, course recorders, engine loggers and computer data.

Moreover, unlike this very generalised foreword, Phil Anderson's book sets out detailed advice relating to many different but foreseeable problems, including cargo claims, loss and damage giving rise to claims against underwriters, charterparty disputes such as speed and warranty claims, bunker disputes, unsafe port claims, pollution, general average, collisions, labour disputes and personal injury claims.

In my judgement (which I should warn the reader is not always held to be reliable by the Court of Appeal), every officer, superintendent, agent, consultant, lawyer, arbitrator and judge should have a copy. I am pleased to have been sent a draft and am hoping to receive the finished article.

Anthony Clarke

FOREWORD II

Captain E.H. Beetham, FRSA, FNI, President, The Nautical Institute.

I hope you never have to use this book, but if you do you will find it most valuable for the practical advice it gives when things go wrong. The benefit however is in reading it first.

Shipping cargoes across the oceans of the world in all weathers, visiting strange ports, working with and relying on people you have never met before, inevitably involves loss and damage at some time.

Similarly, while I hope it never happens, there is always the risk of collision, the unforeseen circumstances which lead to a grounding or the over heavy berthing which can lead to contact damage.

The industry expects that when claims are made they will be settled on the basis of the evidence presented. The need to provide this evidence is part of the mariners' professional role.

The Nautical Institute recognises this and thanks to the pioneering work of the North East Branch, is now the leading authority on this subject. Fortuitously in Newcastle there are a group of vibrant members working on ships in different companies sailing under different flags, carrying a variety of dry and liquid cargoes.

In addition there are four P&I Clubs who have generously worked together to pool their collective wisdom and this had enabled a much deeper appreciation of the shipowners' interests to be articulated.

Finally there a number of law firms, whose clients come from opposing sides of a dispute who have been able to identify the underlying principles upon which claims are settled. It must be noted here that good evidence will often enable a claim to be settled by correspondence which is infinitely preferable to a lengthy and costly court case based upon insubstantial opinion.

A book of this type has to be conceived and to put it together requires leadership. We find this leader in Mr. Philip Anderson, FNI who perhaps not surprisingly is currently the Chairman of the North East Branch. Having worked as an expert witness and as a consultant for plaintiffs and defendants I can say that this one publication has saved shipowners more money than any other I know. The industry owes a debt of gratitude to Mr. Anderson and the team who produced this book.

The Mariner's Role in Collecting Evidence started out as The Masters Role in Collecting Evidence, but the name was changed when it was realised that everybody on board has a positive role to play in accident reporting and loss prevention. To identify just the Master, who probably signs the final report, as the only person involved would be wrong. It is more likely that the watchkeeping officers are going to see the damaged cargo first or witness a personal injury. As such everybody on board must be involved.

A book of this type needs to be updated to reflect changes in the law, new developments like the ISM Code and better practices, as they become part of the shipping culture. This new volume includes a number of substantial and helpful amendments.

A new initiative to help promote this important message is the production of a video. It is cleverly done with animations illustrating the tendency to not bother and real life footage of incidents demonstrating how professionals should behave. The consequences of bad practices come out vividly in a court scene where an officer who lacked diligence is cross examined and humiliated.

Like all good training I am pleased to say there is a similar sequence where the same officer did everything properly and a real sense of professional pride is conveyed. This is an imaginative and effective video which will enhance awareness. When linked to this volume both a sense, purpose and the achievement of results can be realised. Details on how to obtain the video are contained on the back page.

Sea staff have the responsibility of ensuring that cargoes are loaded, carried and discharged in good order and on time.

There can be no doubt that this practical book should be available on all ships and owners would be well advised to encourage their officers to read it and use it when needed. A number of companies have incorporated this book in their standing orders and say 'evidence should be collected in accordance with ...'. That is a testimonial in its own right and recognition of the particular value of the work of those who have contributed to this publication.

Eric Beetham

CONTENTS

Introduction

Background

The Mariner's Role

Layout

Guidelines

Log Books

Operational Records

Informal Notes

Photographs and Videos

Master's Report and the Doctrine of Privilege

Legal Professional Privilege

Self-incriminating Document

The Report

Involvement of Lawyers and other Consultants

Dealing with the Media

The ISM Code

Contributors: Mr Angus Campbell
Capt Andy Cook
Capt David F Heaselden
Capt Savraj Mehta
Capt Mark Rawson
Mr John Reece
Capt Bob Ridge
Capt David Robinson
Mr Mike Salthouse

The Video

A video, also titled "The Mariner's Role in Collecting Evidence", is available to complement this book. Copies can be obtained from the head office of The Nautical Institute, 202 Lambeth Road, London SE1 7LQ.

Members of the working group who contributed to the editing and production of the video:

Capt Phil Anderson
Capt Rod Lingard
Mr Jeremy Webb

A special thanks are also given to the following for their assistance in the making of the video:

- Mr John Bird - Producer

- P&O Ferrymasters

The Management, the Master, Officers and crew on board MV "Elk"
- Souter Shipping Limited

The Management, Officers and crew on board MV "Jostelle" and M.V. "Exemplar"
- Capt James Jamieson

- Mr Angus Campbell

- Capt Kenneth Greest

- Commander Nicholas Iliopoulos

- Capt Paul Bennett

- Mr Richard Shaw

- Mr Michael James

- Mr David Wareing

- Mr Eamon Moloney

- Capt Savraj Mehta

- Chief Officer Philip Curran

- Mr Richard Rayfield

- Capt Alistair Watson

- Mr Matthew Moore

Additional Credits

Special thanks are also extended to:

- The Hon Mr Justice Clarke
  Admiralty Judge
  Admiralty Court
  Royal Courts of Justice – London and to Captain E.H. Beetham President
  The Nautical Institute for providing the forewords to this second edition
- Mrs Paula Owsnett and Mrs Moira Gill – Secretaries to the Chairman for their labour in preparing the final manuscript

- The secretary and staff of the head office of The Nautical Institute for all their help and support throughout.

HOW TO USE THIS BOOK

Introduction

Legal disputes involving the vessel are amongst the many risks inherent in the business of owning and operating ships. Owners' success in these disputes may depend almost entirely on the availability of contemporaneous evidence from the vessel. In cases where the relevant information and documents are available, claims can usually be resolved quickly, avoiding lengthy legal wrangles and crippling legal costs. In the event that claims are brought before a court of tribunal, judges and arbitrators place great weight upon documentation and other contemporaneous evidence from a vessel. If good, clear, and methodical records are produced, the judges and arbitrators will infer that the vessel was operated in a "seamanlike" manner and are more likely to come to a decision in favour of the shipowner.

A few years ago, a number of lawyers and insurance claims handlers involved in the shipping community realised that the evidence required to properly defend claims brought against a vessel frequently was inadequate or not available. One reason for this lack of evidence was that ship's personnel, through no fault of their own, often were unaware of the type of evidence required from the vessel, and, more importantly, were unaware why that evidence was required.

"The Mariner's Role in Collecting Evidence" is an attempt to remedy this problem. The main objective of this work is to guide Masters and officers to adopt a systematic approach in collecting together all the necessary and factual information which may be required to resolve particular claims and disputes which arise during the course of a voyage, and to explain why that evidence is relevant.

Background

The initial problem which was encountered in putting together this work was how the technical and legal requirements of evidence could be expressed accurately and still be of practical use to ship's personnel in the front line. The solution was to solicit the active participation of people from all areas of the shipping community in producing the document.

"The Mariner's Role in Collecting Evidence" has now been completely revised by a newly-formed standing committee in order to take into account recent changes in the law and commercial practice. The committee is satisfied that the work is both legally and commercially accurate and is in a form which will readily be understood by ship's personnel and will be capable of being used onboard any well-run vessel.

The mariner's role

This book is intended to give general guidance to Mariners and should be used together with the standing instructions given by the vessel's operators. This work was not written with the intention that the Master and officers should replace lawyers, surveyors, and other consultants in assembling evidence. Masters and officers have an important role to play in the collecting of evidence.

Firstly, they will be of assistance to lawyers, surveyors, or other consultants instructed by ship owners and their insurers to go on board the vessel to investigate an incident. When an incident occurs, a significant period of time may elapse before the lawyer or surveyor is able to come on board the vessel. In that period of time, valuable information may be destroyed or lost inadvertently. The Master and officers can ensure that they gather together all the relevant information and documents for the lawyer or surveyor to examine when they finally arrive. In addition, they can interview witnesses immediately after the incident while memories are still fresh. The assistance of the Master and officers will make the job of the lawyer or surveyor far easier, will save a considerable amount of time, and will go a long way to ensuring that as thorough an investigation as possible is carried out.

Secondly, there are many minor incidents and disputes which arise during the normal course of a vessel's trading. These may not develop into claims for a considerable time after the incident occurred. The costs involved in investigating such claims by engaging lawyers or other consultants can be disproportionate to the amount at stake. Although the claims may be relatively small, they tend to arise often and, collectively, they represent a substantial amount of money. Therefore, the information recorded by the Master and officers on a regular and routine basis will be essential in defending these claims.

Finally, an increased awareness of the type of evidence required to defend a claim will also lead to an increased awareness of potential problems which could arise on a vessel, and therefore, could lead to greater care being taken by the Master and officers in operating the vessel.

Layout

This work is not, and was never intended to be, a legal text book. However, the subjects discussed involve legal issues and, where relevant, brief explanations of the legal concepts are provided.

Furthermore, the work does not attempt to cover every possible type of claim which could arise, but concentrates on the more frequently occurring incidents. However, if the Master is familiar with the general approach put forward in this work, he should be in a position to work out for himself what evidence is required in all types of incidents.

This work has been prepared for use on board any type of merchant vessel of any nationality. Although attempts have been made to keep the advice and recommendations general, the legal concepts are based on English law (however, in Chapter ten, a Greek lawyer was consulted to provide a comparative discussion on labour disputes and disciplinary problems under Greek law).

The main body of this work is divided into fourteen chapters. Guidelines are provided which will be generally applicable to each of the chapters. Each chapter includes a discussion on the nature of the problems which are likely to arise in the particular subject, the type of evidence required, and why that evidence is important. The committee, as far as possible, has avoided making reference to specific court cases or legislation.

Where relevant, checklists have been provided to assist the Master in assembling the evidence. Although the lists are not exhaustive, they have been made as comprehensive as possible. These lists are merely guidelines. Particular circumstances will dictate which items are relevant. In all cases, the Master and officers will have to consider what additional information will be required to present a complete record of a particular incident.

Where appropriate, a case history has also been included. The case histories are all based on actual court or arbitration hearings. Case histories are most useful as they demonstrate the value placed on the evidence from the vessel which either helped the shipowner defend the action, or, in cases where the relevant evidence was lacking, contributed to the shipowner being held liable by the court or tribunal.

Guidelines

Certain items of evidence, such as log books, Master's reports and notebooks, photographs and videos, are of fundamental importance in the investigation of any type of incident which may occur on board a vessel. This chapter examines how these documents or information should be prepared. In addition, this chapter examines the doctrine of privilege and its effect on reports prepared by the Master.

An outline of this chapter is as follows:

Log books

Operational records

Informal notes

Photographs and videos

The Master's report and the doctrine of privilege -
   Legal professional privilege
   Self-incriminating documents
   The report

The involvement of lawyers and other consultants.

Log books

A number of different types of log books will be kept on board every vessel. These will include the official log, the deck or mate's log, the engine room log, rough logs, as well as the radio log, and sick bay log. For the purposes of this book, the official log, the rough log, the deck or mate's log, and the engine room log are the most important.

Judges and arbitrators place great weight on these logs as a contemporaneous record of the vessel. Therefore, it is of paramount importance that all log books are maintained in an orderly manner and fully and accurately record all relevant factual information. Movement books, bell books, course recorder print-outs or any other type of rough logs are also important items of evidence and should be maintained in a neat and orderly manner.

The Master should ensure that the officers and crew are aware of the importance of a log book and take care in making entries. Entries in the log books should always be written neatly and legibly in ink. If a mistake is made, a single line should be drawn through the relevant passage. Words should never be erased, either by rubbing out, or by painting with erasing fluid. Erasures appear suspicious when log books are examined by the opposing party to a dispute, and, in any event, techniques are available whereby words which have been erased can be read. Furthermore, a judge or arbitrator examining a log book which has many erasures and is untidy may draw adverse inferences about the way a vessel is generally operated.

Operational records

Any well run vessel keeps many operational records for example:

- Crew overtime sheets

- Maintenance reports

- Daily workbooks

- Life saving and fire fighting appliances (LSA & FFA) maintenance books

- Fire and safety drill books

- Requisition sheets for spare parts

- Oil record book

- Garbage disposal records

These operational records can be important as a supplement to the brief log book entries and can help to form a more complete picture of events onboard.

Informal notes

masters and officers often keep informal contemporaneous notes or in some cases diaries of events on board. These notes are of great evidential value. In particular, if a Master or officer is called before a court or tribunal to give evidence, he may read passages from his notes in support of his oral evidence.

However, if any part of his notes are relied upon as evidence, the entire notes must be made available to all the parties to legal proceedings. Therefore, the Master should ensure that his notes are of an objective and factual nature and should avoid giving his personal views which, in the event that his notes are made available to the other parties to legal proceedings, may embarrass the Master and the owners and may even adversely affect the owners' case.

Photographs and videos

As the case history in the appendix to Chapter one demonstrates, photographs and videos can provide essential evidence. In one instance, for example, owners were able to defeat a claim for cargo shortage by producing as evidence photographs that showed a cargo of grain, which had been discharged into road trucks, spilling out of the back gate of the trucks. Photographs and video can also show heavy weather conditions, inadequate fendering, how cargo was secured, or the general condition of the vessel. Similarly, sketches and drawings are of immense value in depicting certain incidents.

If possible, photographs, videos, or sketches should be used to support the Master's written report. They should be clearly labelled to identify the ship or subject, indicate the date, time and place and initialled by the Master. Some cameras and video recorders will now automatically record the date and time.

Master's reports and the doctrine of privilege

A Master of a vessel is likely to prepare a report whenever the vessel is involved in an incident which may give rise to legal proceedings. In the event that legal proceedings ensue, the report will be of clear evidential value to all the other parties to the legal proceedings. This section deals with the question of whether a Master's report must be produced to all parties to the proceedings or whether it may be exempt from such production as a "privileged" document.

English arbitration and court proceedings are conducted on the basis that each party to an action submits evidence in support of their case. The general rule is that the parties to the proceedings must disclose and produce all relevant documents. In this context "disclosed" means that the existence of the documents must be made known. "Produced" means that they must be made available for inspection. The one exception to the general rule is that documents which are privileged are exempt from production (although not disclosure). In some other jurisdictions, the rules in relation to production of all relevant documents are even stricter than in England.

A Master's report is relevant to legal proceedings and may be used by the other parties to the proceedings as evidence unless it is privileged. The report may be privileged on the ground of legal professional privilege or on the ground that it is a self-incriminating document.

Legal professional privilege

Legal professional privilege arises as a result of the need for a legal advisor to gather evidence and examine the issues relevant to a case without the fear of prejudicing a client's interest in the proceedings. All correspondence between a legal advisor and his client is privileged provided that it is written to or by the legal advisor for the purpose of giving legal advice or assistance. A Master's report will be protected from production if it is prepared by a Master subsequent to an incident likely to give rise to litigation proceedings, and if it is prepared for the purpose of obtaining legal advice and is addressed solely to the owners' legal advisors.

In recent times, it has become common practice for Masters to submit accident

14

"confidential report for the information only of the company's legal advisors prepared for the purpose of obtaining professional advice in proceedings pending, threatened, or anticipated".

Such an endorsement will not of itself protect the document from production as it is the purpose for which the report was produced which will determine whether or not it is privileged. However, it will assist in demonstrating that the requirements, by reason of which privilege may be claimed, are fulfilled. If the report is so endorsed, it should be submitted directly to the owners' legal advisors.

Despite the likelihood that the Master's report may not be privileged on the ground that it is routinely prepared, a report prepared contemporaneously to an incident which may be the subject of legal proceedings is an invaluable document. Such a report would provide owners and their legal advisors with a complete account of the events surrounding the incident and allow them to prepare fully for legal proceedings. The evidential value of such a document, therefore, clearly outweighs the possible risks that the report will be used as evidence by the other parties to legal proceedings.

Self-incriminating document

A Master's report may also be privileged from production on the ground that it would incriminate or expose the Master or owners to criminal proceedings in the United Kingdom. Although a Master's report will rarely be incriminating, the doctrine of self-incrimination may be significant in the context of criminal proceedings under the Merchant Shipping Acts. Privilege may only be claimed if the risk of incrimination is real.

The report

In view of the likelihood that the Master's report will have to be made available to all parties to legal proceedings, the report should be limited to a factual and objective account of the incident (the following chapters provide guidelines on the type of information which should be included in the report in particular cases). The Master, as far as possible, should avoid giving his opinions on how an incident occurred. For the purposes of investigating the incident, the Master's views are extremely important. However, they will be taken into account at the appropriate time and should not be included in his report. The Master should also avoid entering into a discussion about the incident in the general voyage report to owners as that document will almost certainly be made available to all the parties.

Involvement of lawyers and other consultants

In the aftermath of a major incident, it is usual for all the interested parties to send lawyers or other consultants on board the vessel to collect evidence and ascertain the true sequence of events. Before admitting these persons on board the vessel, the

Master and officers should identify who these persons are and whom they represent, and, if possible, should seek authorisation from owners or their local agents. Finally, the Master should ensure that the officers and crew do not discuss the incident with anybody who questions them (or in general) without the prior authorisation of owners or their agents.

Dealing with the media

Following a major accident or incident, mariners should be aware that statements made by crew members to the media may be inadvertently used out of context and prejudice the legal position of the owners or simply result in bad publicity for the vessel. Therefore, following such incidents all enquiries from the media should be directed to owners' media spokesperson.

The ISM Code

With the introduction of the ISM Code there will be established, within every shipping company and on board every ship, various procedures for producing documentation and reports. The guidelines contained within "The Mariner's Role in Collecting Evidence" may be helpful when considering how many of the documents and reports are compiled.

The relevance of the Code

The "International Management Code for the Safe Operation of Ships and for Pollution Prevention" (ISM Code), was adopted by IMO Resolution A741(18) and given mandatory effect by its adoption into Solas 74, Chapter IX. The development of the ISM Code, as with most marine safety legislation flows from well known casualties with significant loss of life. During the inquiry into the loss of the *Herald of Free Enterprise* an apparent dislocation of authority and responsibility between the shore based and ship based management was noted that was considered to have been a contributory factor in the events that led to the loss of this vessel. Increasing amounts of statistical evidence indicating that the human element played a significant part in the majority of marine casualties also encouraged the International Maritime Organisation to introduce quality management techniques to the operation of ships.

The ISM Code requires assessment of both the shore based and ship board management systems. On board ship a Safety Management System (SMS) will need to meet the requirements of the ISM Code by documenting the management and operational procedures, and providing evidence that these procedures, particularly those involving safety and protection of the environment, have been followed.

All mariners will be involved with operating to the requirements of the ISM Code during their day to day duties. There is no direct requirement within the ISM Code for the mariner to collect evidence in the event of an accident, casualty, damage to property or other unforeseen occurrence. However, the need to collect evidence overlaps with certain sections of the code and should be covered in the companies Safety Management System (SMS).

By effective implementation of the Code it is intended that a safety culture will develop providing safe practices in ship operation and thus a safer working environment. The company should develop instructions and procedures for key shipboard operations relating to safety and pollution prevention in order to "continuously improve safety management skills both ashore and afloat" (ISM Code 1.2.2.3).

The Code details how these objectives are to be met with the role of the Mariner in collecting and maintaining evidence described in sections 8, 9, 10 and 11.

Section 10 of the code deals with maintenance of the ship and equipment, requiring that maintenance procedures are established, non-conformities and corrective action is taken and that specific measures are taken to identify and prevent the failure of identified pieces of equipment; where a sudden operational failure may result in a hazardous situation. As in all quality management systems inspections are to be held and records are to be maintained.

Section 9 of the Code is concerned with procedures that are to be established, and included within the SMS for ensuring that non-conformities, accidents and hazardous situations are reported and that corrective action is implemented in line with established procedures.

The principle of reporting, analysing and learning from near misses and hazardous occurrences has been recognised and found to be beneficial in many industries. Working to a management standard makes it clear that investigations are required to be undertaken by shore and ship's staff. To be effective these investigations should be frank and honest with a view to preventing a re-occurrence of the particular incident, however, this can lead to a certain conflict of interests when the incident ends up as a legal dispute between the company and another party.

For instance an 'Accident/Hazardous Situation Report' form set up for a company's safety management system, should have sections in place outlining details of investigations and detailing any corrective and 'follow-up' actions. With a dispute pending, legal experts may want mariners to be more selective and only include the facts of the case. Documents detailing any corrective action may be evidence that the initial incident was caused by a failure to follow procedures or that the procedure itself was flawed. The implications of this requirement when defending a claim will only become clear in time.

The above requirements could be considered to fall under the general heading of corrective action and preventative measures to ensure that these occurrences do not happen again. Section 8 of the ISM Code includes details of the actions to be taken and the procedures to follow in the event of an emergency situation developing. The company should establish procedures to identify, describe and respond to potential emergency situations, including establishing procedures for drills and exercises and responses to emergencies.

Section 11.1 of the ISM code requires the company to establish and maintain procedures to control all documents which are relevant to the SMS. Within any SMS there should be procedures for maintaining important documents correctly. Such documents would include amongst others:

Official log book	Deck log book
Engine room log book	Maintenance records
Movement books	Oil record book
Ship's certificates	Cargo documentation
Stability data	Crew agreements
Bunker records	Accident report forms
Casualty reports	Port Information

The importance of keeping accurate records cannot be overstated. Even in normal operating conditions mariners may face problems if they fail to comply with this requirement. For example, incorrect oil record book entries can easily lead to fines or detention by Port State Control inspections. Documentation control is one of the fundamentals of any quality system and records will need to be produced for audit during future ISM Code assessments.

Following an incident, evidence will be collected as part of the investigation and the importance of having well maintained documents will be obvious. For example, log books and movement books should provide factual evidence of events leading up to, during and following an incident.

If the company is operating a management system to the requirements of the quality assurance standard ISO 9002, then in addition non-conformities will be raised for customer complaints, such as cargo damage, loss or shortage as well as under performance and over consumption claims.

The mariner must be aware that each incident is unique and may have to be handled in a different way. However, it must be stressed that in safety and pollution issues the over-riding consideration is with the prevention of re-occurrence of an incident.

In summary, a good SMS complying with the requirements of the ISM Code will have aspects contained in it that relate to the collection of evidence following an incident. Technical publications can be referred to in a SMS and therefore form part of the companies' overall system. "The Mariner's Role in Collecting Evidence" is thus a valuable part of any company's technical library to be referred to ashore and afloat.

Chapter One

CARGO DAMAGE, LOSS AND SHORTAGE

Introduction

The most fundamental principle underlying the carriage of goods by sea is that the carrier (a term which almost always includes the shipowner) is entrusted with another person's property to transport it from one place to another. Therefore, if the cargo is lost or damaged in transit, the carrier will have to account for that loss or damage. The contracts under which goods are carried generally determine the obligations and responsibilities of the carrier. In respect of any one voyage, there may be several related contracts. Sometimes the terms of all the contracts are consistent but often they will conflict with each other. In order to properly defend a claim for cargo damage, loss or shortage, the carrier must be able to demonstrate that he has fulfilled his obligations under the governing contract(s) of carriage, that the vessel was in an efficient state and that the cargo was cared for properly.

An outline of this chapter is as follows:

The fixture

The ship
    A seaworthy ship
    The exercise of due diligence

The cargo

The bill of lading

The voyage

The claim

Evidence required from the vessel
    Documentary Evidence
    The Master's Report

In the appendix to this chapter a case history is provided.

The fixture

A charterparty and bill of lading often represent two separate contracts in relation to the same voyage. Both of the contracts may be relevant and the Master and the shipowner may have to show what they have done to comply with the terms of the contracts. Therefore, it is essential that the Master is familiar with the terms of all of the contracts applying to a particular voyage and with local practices and regulations which affect the performance of these contracts. The Master will be able to obtain information about the contracts from owners and charterers and obtain information about local custom from owners' local agents and P&I correspondents. It is also important that the Master is aware of the instructions issued by the charterers and keeps a careful record of all instructions issued in respect of the voyage.

International conventions, especially the Hague Rules/Hague-Visby Rules and Hamburg Rules, attempt to arrive at a common approach to some of the basic issues in relation to the carriage of goods. Many contracts of carriage incorporate either the Hague Rules or the Hague-Visby Rules (the differences between the two being of little practical importance to good cargo practice) and the obligations and responsibilities imposed on the carrier by these Rules provide the framework for this chapter.

The ship

If cargo is lost or damaged, there is a presumption that the carrier has not taken care to ensure the ship is in a thoroughly efficient state. The Hague and Hague-Visby Rules impose an obligation to exercise due diligence to make the ship seaworthy.

A seaworthy ship

A seaworthy cargo ship is one which can take its cargo to sea without risk of danger and damage to either the ship or the cargo arising out of the ordinary marine environment or the failure of the ship. The concept of seaworthiness extends beyond the integrity of the vessel's hull and machinery. The vessel must be properly equipped and manned with a competent crew who are well trained in all shipboard procedures. The vessel must be in good condition and must have everything it requires in order to perform properly.

The exercise of due diligence

The Hague and Hague-Visby Rules require the carrier to exercise due diligence to make the ship seaworthy before it puts to sea. Exercising due diligence means taking good care.

If problems arise on board during the course of a voyage, the test for determining whether or not the carrier has taken good care to make the ship seaworthy is as follows:

- Should the defect have come to light by the careful checking of the ship before the voyage began?

- If so, would a careful owner have mended that defect before sending the ship, with her cargo on board, to sea?

In order to ensure that good care has been taken, there is no substitute for the proper and regular checking of all aspects of the ship and its manning, of all work, maintenance, and repairs carried out on board. Moreover, all procedures and standing instructions which are in force on board should be reviewed in order to ensure that these are adequate and well suited for the ship putting to sea and safely carrying her cargo. All checks and regular maintenance work should be carried out as often as necessary to avoid failure in the vessel, its personnel or its procedures.

The reader is referred to the Introduction (How to use this Book) dealing with the ISM Code, the implementation of which will necessarily involve a thorough review of shipboard procedures.

The Master and the crew should not rely on the findings of the outside examiners such as classification society or underwriters' surveyors. These surveyors have different interests and do not usually work to the same guidelines, standards or requirements.

All of the checks and regular maintenance work carried out by the crew should be properly recorded and documented. If something does go wrong and cargo is lost or damaged, then the presumption will be that the carrier has not taken good care to make the vessel seaworthy. In order to refute this presumption, the carrier must have evidence in the form of log books, work schedules, work books, work specifications, accounts, standing instructions, reports and contemporaneous correspondence to show that good care has been taken to make the vessel seaworthy.

The cargo

In addition to the obligation to take good care to make the ship seaworthy, the Rules also impose an obligation on the carrier to take good care to look after the cargo from the time it is entrusted to him until the time that it is delivered to the receiver (see Hague Rules, Article III, rule 2). If the cargo, at the time of delivery, is lost or damaged, the carrier will be called upon to explain how the loss or damage occurred.

The period of time during which the carrier must take good care of the cargo can only be determined by looking at many different factors. The relevant contracts (for example, the charterparty and bill of lading) will usually determine the period of time during which the carrier remains responsible for the cargo. However, local laws may override or refuse to recognise contractual provisions which conflict with local regulations or practice.

The obligation on the carrier is to do everything necessary to deliver the cargo to the receiver in **as good condition** as when it was entrusted to the carrier. The carrier, therefore, must ensure that all cargo handling operations, including the loading, stowing, carrying, and discharging, are done properly and carefully. Moreover, the carrier must ensure that the cargo is properly cared for and kept so that the condition of the cargo is maintained. The Master should be fully aware of any special attention that the cargo may require. Information and instructions with regard to the treatment of cargo should be sought in writing from the shipper. If the Master has any reservations about this information, he should request the assistance of the shipowner or their local agents who may appoint an independent surveyor or expert. The Master should ensure that all the crew members are also aware of their individual responsibilities concerning the cargo operations, in particular, with regard to the supervision and control of stevedores and the stowage and securing of the cargo.

The carrier may be held responsible for any problems which arise out of any of the cargo handling operations which he has contracted to undertake or arrange. In addition, the carrier will be held responsible for any cargo handling operations for which, under the local laws, he is primarily responsible, whether or not he has contractually undertaken to do these operations. Therefore, it is essential that the Master is aware of the local laws, custom, and practices as well as the provisions in the relevant contracts which relate to cargo handling operations. The owners' local agents or local P&I correspondents should be able to advise him of local laws which dictate that particular cargo operations fall within the carrier's responsibility.

If a particular cargo handling operation, which is the carrier's responsibility, is not carried out properly, the carrier will be unable to avoid liability if loss or damage occurs to the cargo even if the Master inserts into the statement of facts an endorsement stating that the carrier is not responsible. Such endorsements may be of evidential value for indemnity proceedings and the Master may note on the statement of facts or in correspondence any irregularities relating to the cargo handling operations.

The standard of care required of the carrier is independent of the usual custom or practice. The carrier's obligation is to look after the cargo properly and carefully and it will be of no defence to a claim for damage to say that the cargo was carried in accordance with usual practice.

In order to avoid liability if cargo is lost or damaged, the carrier will have to demonstrate that his obligation of caring for the cargo (during loading and discharging operations as well as during the voyage) has been fully and properly discharged. Therefore, the Master must ensure that all cargo handling operations are accurately recorded and fully documented so that the carrier will be able to bring forward the evidence necessary to defend a claim. Contemporary evidence relating to loading and discharging operations may be vital in successfully defeating a cargo claim. For example, the evidence may demonstrate that cargo was never loaded or that it was damaged at a time by someone for whom the shipowner is not responsible. Even if the shipowner has to, in the first instance, pay the claim, the contemporary evidence may assist him in claiming an indemnity from a third party who is responsible for the damage.

The bill of lading

From the viewpoint of both the carrier and the shipper, documents which demonstrate the amount and the condition of cargo carried on the ship are essential. The bill of lading is the most important of such documents. The Hague and Hague-Visby Rules provide for the bill of lading to be a record of the **quantity of cargo and its apparent order and condition** at the time the cargo is entrusted to carrier's care and responsibility (see Hague Rules, Article III, rule 3).

Without ever having seen the cargo, prospective buyers often decide to purchase goods on the basis of the description in the bill of lading. If bills of lading are issued which inaccurately describe the cargo, the consequences may be extremely costly for the carrier. Therefore, it is essential that all the information on the face of the bill of lading is checked carefully.

The carrier is under an obligation to verify the amount of cargo and to verify its condition and identifying marks at the time the cargo comes into his custody and care. The Master should ensure that all the proper arrangements are made for this purpose and should seek clarification from the shipowner if they have not been made.

The carrier will be unable to avoid liabilities which arise as a result of a failure to check the cargo unless a check is not reasonably possible. Furthermore, endorsements on the bill of lading, such as "shipper's figures", "figures as per shore tally", "quantity and condition unknown", or "said to be...", will seldom absolve the carrier of blame if he was able, but has failed to check the particulars of the cargo to his own satisfaction.

The Master should not state anything in the bill of lading which he believes to be inaccurate. If the bill of lading does contain inaccurate information, the Master should correct it with an appropriate clause before signing it. If the shippers and/or the charterers insist that bills of lading are issued which do not accurately reflect the quantity or condition of the cargo or the date it was loaded, it is essential that the Master obtain clear instructions and advice from the shipowner and his P&I Club lawyers.

In addition to the bill of lading, there are many other documents which record the quantity and condition of the cargo. The mate's receipt, cargo manifest, stowage plans, tallies, and draft surveys, as well as notebooks, correspondence, and reports are all of great evidential value. The carrier will rely on such documents to demonstrate the condition and quantity of the cargo at the time it was entrusted to him and defend any claim for loss or damage.

The voyage

The carrier, having provided a seaworthy vessel which is fit to go to sea with her cargo on board and having received the cargo into his care, must perform the voyage dictated by the contract of carriage. Under the Hague and Hague-Visby Rules, the carrier is obliged, in the absence of any agreement to the contrary, to carry the cargo directly to its destination (see Hague Rules, Article IV, rule 4).

Therefore, the route of the voyage is crucial to the proper fulfilment of the contract of carriage. Any unjustifiable deviation from the agreed, direct, or customary route will constitute a breach of the contract of carriage and may jeopardise the shipowner's P&I insurance cover. **A deviation** is justifiable in only three situations.

Firstly, if there is a real or immediate danger, the carrier may deviate for the purpose of protecting and preserving the cargo. In certain circumstances, if the well being of the cargo so demands, it may be the carrier's duty to deviate.

Secondly, the carrier may deviate for the purpose of saving human life. However, he may not unnecessarily delay the vessel at the scene of a casualty.

Finally, the contract of carriage may permit a deviation from the contractual voyage if it contains a "liberty to deviate" clause. It is not safe to rely on such clauses as they are interpreted in a most narrow and restrictive manner. The Hague and Hague-Visby Rules, which will usually be incorporated into the contract of carriage, excuse deviations for the purpose of saving life and/or property, or for any other reasonable purpose. It is virtually impossible to define what is meant by

23

reasonable. However, the question of whether a deviation is reasonable will be considered not only from the point of view of the carrier but from the point of view of the cargo owners as well.

The carrier is also under an obligation to ensure that the vessel proceeds promptly to her destination. The duration of the voyage is crucial to the proper fulfilment of the contract of carriage, and any unnecessary delay will be treated in the same way as a deviation from the contractual voyage.

In the event the vessel deviates from the agreed, direct, or customary route, or in the event of delay in the prosecution of the voyage, the Master should notify the shipowner immediately. In addition he should ensure that the precise and detailed reasons for the deviation or delay are fully and accurately recorded, and documents such as the log book, ship to shore communications, course recorders, and charts must be made available to owners.

The claim

The main objective of the Hague and Hague-Visby Rules is to ensure that the cargo is delivered **in like good order and condition** which means that the condition of the cargo should not have deteriorated whilst it was in the care and custody of the carrier. However, the Rules recognise the possibility that, for reasons beyond the control of the carrier, he may fail to meet that obligation.

In such cases, the Rules may protect the carrier from liability for claims arising out of his failure to deliver the cargo "in like good order and condition" (see Hague Rules, Article IV, rules 1-2). However, before he can rely on these exceptions the carrier must fulfil all of his obligations under the Rules. The carrier, in seeking to defend a claim for cargo loss or damage, must first demonstrate that he has exercised due diligence to make the ship seaworthy and that he has properly kept and cared for the cargo. If the carrier fails to show that he has fulfilled these obligations, he will not be able to rely on the exceptions.

The reader should note three important points relating to the Rules. Firstly, the exceptions will only come to the aid of the carrier if he has done everything possible to look after the cargo and prevent loss or damage occurring. Secondly, the scope of the exceptions are continually diminishing; the carrier is expected to learn not only from his own mistakes but also from those of other carriers within the shipping community. Thirdly, as with the deviation provisions, the exceptions are interpreted in a narrow and restrictive sense and the carrier can never rely on them confidently.

The obligations imposed on the carrier by the Rules have been devised to keep loss and damage to a minimum. Thus, it is likely that where cargo loss and damage has arisen, the carrier will be found to have been in breach of the Rules. This does not mean that the carrier will be found liable for every cargo claim brought against him. However, the carrier will be in a far better position to defend claims and to produce the evidence required to refute them if he has implemented, in the first instance, the very systems and procedures on board the vessel which minimise the risks of claims arising.

Evidence required from the vessel

Documentary Evidence

In a claim for cargo loss or damage, the documents listed below should be assembled whenever possible and numbered in consecutive order. They should then be referred to in the Master's report which is discussed in the next section. It is recognised that in certain instances these documents will be more easily available from the shipowner's office, but if they are available on the vessel and attached to the report they will be of great assistance in limiting the amount of commentary which has to be included in the report. The documents are as follows:

- A convenient plan of the vessel which includes a description of the distribution of hatches and holds, the position of the vessel's equipment, the distribution of double bottom tanks, wing tanks and peak tanks and capacities;
- Vessel's tonnage certificate;
- Class certificates including recommendations, reservations, and conditions of class at the time of the loss or incident;
- Crew list;
- Reports of the Master or deck or engineer officers on regular inspection and maintenance of the vessel and her equipment;
- Standing orders for regular inspection and maintenance of vessel prior to sailing;
- Inspection, repair, and maintenance schedules;
- Inspection, repair, and maintenance logs;
- Repair and maintenance accounts;
- Records of steel thickness;
- Shipboard management system, owner's verification records, internal and external audit records;
- Corrections and maintenance records for nautical publications;
- Technical manuals and operators' manuals;
- Repair records from outside contractors;
- Condition reports;
- Crew documents, qualifications certificates of competency, manning certificates;
- Certificate of fitness (chemical and gas carriers);
- Cargo system and auxiliary system test and calibration records;
- Performance/specification/manufacturer's date of cargo handling equipment/ systems;
- Vessel's deadweight/freeboard calculations;
- Vessel's calculation of bending moments in various stages of employment;

- Stability calculations;
- Mate's receipts;
- Bills of lading;
- Charterparty(-ies);
- Draft surveys with all accompanying calculations;
- Letters of protest;
- Deck log abstracts for the period of loaded voyage including loading and discharging operations and the period or voyage before loading if, during this time, heavy weather was encountered or hold cleaning was carried out;
- Ventilation records if not included in the deck log;
- Temperature records if not included in the deck log;
- Bilge sounding records if not included in the deck log;
- Engine logs for the same period;
- Statement of facts at load and discharge port;
- Time sheets at load and discharge port;
- Notice of readiness at load and discharge port;
- Tally sheets at load and discharge port;
- Cargo manifest;
- Cargo preparation procedures and records;
- Inspection records, surveyor's reports, draft survey calculations prior to loading;
- Cargo handling equipment test records;
- Cargo isolation/segregation procedures and diagrams;
- Cargo log book entries;
- Cargo calculation records before and after loading;
- Cargo security methods and plan;
- Reports of laboratory analyses of cargo samples;
- Hatch closing/sealing procedures;
- Stowage plan (for each port if cargo loaded at several load ports);
- Course recorder printout;
- Echo sounder rolls, engine telegraph recorder;
- Empty Hold Certificate;
- Integrated bridge system printouts;
- Cargo/ballast/fuel records;
- Routine position reports;
- Working chart (with the original markings) if the course or incidents of the voyage were unusual;

- Correspondence with charterers, shippers, ... procedures, supercargo, or any ... of organisation involved in cargo handling operations including pre-arrival notice of readiness, part clearance/health clearance, documentation;

- Copies of all cables or radio messages received by the vessel in particular, demonstrating the weather encountered, contact with other vessels, and Ocean Routeing (or similar) messages;

- Photographs demonstrating the condition of the vessel, weather encountered, methods of loading and discharging of the cargo, and stowage of cargo -

These will greatly enhance owners' case in the event of disputes. In addition, a note should accompany the photographs identifying when they were taken, by whom, and what they purport to depict. The negatives should be carefully preserved

- Videos -

There is an increasing possibility that vessels will carry video equipment, and these can and should be used to identify obvious deficiencies in loading or discharging techniques, methods of stowage, or heavy weather encountered

- Computer printouts -

If the vessel has on board a computer capable of doing stability, draft, and trim calculations, the printouts or recorded disks should be preserved.

Master's Report

Although the Master's report should set out the information in the same order that it is listed below, the Master should ensure that he assembles the contemporaneous evidence first. The Master's Report should include the following information:

1. **Details of the Master -**
   Master's name
   Home address
   Home telephone number
   Age and date of birth
   Qualifications
   Date of Master's certificate and where obtained
   Date of first seagoing experience
   Date when first assumed command of a vessel
   Date when first sailed on present vessel.

2. **Details of the vessel -**
   Vessel's name
   Port of Registry
   Flag
   Type of vessel, for example, 'tween decker, bulk carrier, obo, or other
   LOA

Beam
Summer draught
Gross registered tonnage
Net registered tonnage
Summer DWT
Classification society status
Number of holds, number of hatches, and type of hatch covers
Layout of double bottom, ballast, and peak tanks (prepare diagram if necessary)
Engine model and type
Position of bilge sounding pipes (prepare diagram if necessary)
Position of DBT sounding and overflow pipes (prepare diagram if necessary)
Note whether the vessel has any of the following navigational equipment:
- gyro/magnetic compass
- repeaters on wings
- radar (note the range and type of radar)
- decca/loran
- RDF
- satellite navigation equipment
- echo sounder
- course recorder
- radio equipment including VHF
- anemometer
- other equipment
Vessel's complement.

3. **Details of preliminary voyage to load port -**
   Previous cargo carried
   Weather encountered
   Ballast distribution
   Condition of holds prior to loading (if relevant, include the work done by crew to clean holds)
   Whether or not the bilge pump suction ability was checked on passage or before loading
   Whether or not ballast tanks were pressed up on passage before loading.

4. **Details of loading operation -**
   Name of load port
   Details of pre-arrival notice requirements
   When and where the Notice of Readiness was tendered
   Details of free pratique formalities
   Draft restrictions
   Date(s) of arrival
   Name of loading berth(s)

Time(o) of building

Name of owners' representative, if attending

Name(s) of surveyor(s) if attending and the parties which they represent

Cargo type or types

Whether or not specific instructions were given as to the nature of cargo and method of loading and if so by whom

Details of reporting procedures

Method of loading (ship's equipment, shore equipment, grabs, elevator, or other).

5. **Loading sequence -**

Dates and times when cargo loaded

Quantity loaded

Stoppages

Whether or not a tally was taken of the cargo and if so by whom (ship's agents, charterers' agents, shippers' agents, or deck officer)

Problems involved in loading operations and whether any protests were issued

Details of shippers' documentation procedures

Details of any cargo information obtained or provided.

Whether or not an inspection of the cargo stowage areas had been carried out prior to loading

Whether cargo handling equipment was tested/inspected prior to arrival

Whether necessary isolation procedures or fuel, ballast or other cargo was checked and found effective.

6. **Details of lashing, stowage and trimming -**

Whether or not specific instructions were given, and if so by whom

Whether or not shore labour or equipment was used and if so which companies were involved, and by whom was the shore labour appointed

Whether or not dunnage was used and if so by whom was it provided and what was its nature

Who carried out trimming operations

Who carried out lashing operations

Describe the number and dimension of lashing wires used and points (if necessary prepare a diagram)

Details of draft survey (if any) before commencement and on completion of loading

Whether or not the mate's receipt was claused

Who issued the bills of lading and whether or not they were claused and consistent with the mate's receipt (if not, why not)

Details of the closing of hatches, when were they closed, checked (and by whom) and whether or not any problems were encountered.

7. **Details of loaded voyage** (the following information should be included if it is not apparent from the deck log abstracts or deck log) -

Date of sailing, destination, speed, and course intended

Periods of heavy weather encountered including method of assessment of wind speed, for example, wave observation or anemometer

Changes in course or speed and reasons for the alterations

Wave and sea state on Beaufort scale

Damage suffered by deck fittings and equipment (if any)

Loss of deck fittings and equipment (if any)

Frequency of weather reports received and their accuracy

Whether or not Ocean Routeing or similar service was used

Whether or not the ship was in radio contact with other vessels and if so their names

Ballast distribution on sailing and any changes made or occurring during voyage

Whether or not hatches were opened and if so why and when

Periods during which cargo was ventilated and in which holds

Whether or not readings listed below were taken and if so with what frequency:

- cargo temperatures
- bilge soundings
- seawater temperatures
- air temperatures

Whether or not regular checks had been carried out on the securing of the cargo

Whether or not regular checks had been carried out confirming isolation of the cargo from fuel, ballast and other cargo

Whether or not regular checks had been carried out on the water tightness of hatch covers.

8. **Details of discharging operation** -

Name of and time of arrival at discharge port

Draft survey on arrival

Name and time of berthing at discharge berth

Details of the shore/terminal reception area

Name of attending surveyor

Name of attending supercargo

Name of ship's agent

Whether or not specific instructions were given regarding method of discharge and if so by whom

Type of equipment used and whether it was ship's equipment or shore equipment

Dates and times when cargo discharged

Quantity discharged

Whether or not a tally of the cargo was taken and if so by whom (ship's

agents, charterers' agents, shippers' agents, or deck officer)
Whether or not particular problems were encountered during the discharging operation
Whether or not shore labour was involved and if so what company and by whom was the shore labour appointed.

9. **Details of loss, shortage, or damage -**
When was the first report of loss, shortage, or damage made and by whom and to whom was it sent
Did a joint inspection take place and if so name parties involved, their representatives and note the date of the inspection
Where was cargo discharged and stored
Whether or not any attempt was made to segregate damaged cargo from good cargo and if so
- how was this done
- was the method used agreed by the ship and if not was a protest made
- what is an estimate of the period of delay to the vessel whilst the cargo was being segregated
- was cargo abandoned on deck and if so how much approximately
Weather conditions encountered during discharge
If damage arose as a result of insufficiency of packing, how was the packing deficient and did the equipment used by the stevedores, type of dunnage used, method of stowing or lashing, or general handling of the cargo contribute to the damage.

Illustration

A bulk carrier of about 70,000 DWT was operating under a time charter for one trip from the West coast of the United States to India, and loaded almost a full cargo of bulk wheat.

During the initial stages of the voyage, the vessel encountered severe weather conditions as a result of which there was an ingress of water through the hatch covers which seriously damaged the cargo. Further damage was caused at the discharge port when sound and wet cargo were mixed. A total of nearly 8,000 MT of cargo was affected, and a claim in excess of one and a half million US dollars was brought against the vessel.

The charterers, who were initially liable for the damage, claimed an indemnity from the owners, and the dispute was submitted to arbitration. The owners sought to rely on the Hague Rules' perils of the sea defence. However, the charterers alleged that the owners had failed to exercise due diligence to make the patent hatch covers seaworthy.

The arbitrators held that if the owners had exercised due diligence to make the vessel seaworthy they could successfully rely on the perils of the sea defence because the vessel had encountered severe weather even though the weather was not entirely unexpected or unusual. The arbitrators stated that if this was not correct the defence would never apply to areas like the North Atlantic or North Pacific where severe weather is often encountered in the winter.

In support of their arguments that the weather encountered by the vessel had been severe the owners submitted the vessel's log books as well as a video taken by the Master during the voyage. The log book entries showed that from an early stage in the voyage, the vessel encountered winds of force 6 to 7 from the South East with accompanying rough seas, increasing in strength over the following two days to force 8. The vessel then encountered force 9 winds from the West South West with heavy seas causing the vessel to pitch and roll and ship seas. In the next two days the worst weather was recorded with westerly winds of force 9 to 11 and huge waves. At this stage the vessel had to heave to for about 24 hours and eventually headed south to get away from the violent weather. During this period the vessel suffered damage and well secured drums of lubricant at the stern were carried away. The winds slowly abated to below force 7 during the following two to three day period.

The evidence contained in the log books was supported by a twenty minute video film taken by the Master during the voyage. The arbitrators found that the film did not demonstrate that the weather had been as ferocious as recorded in the log book, but conceded that it was not possible to film during the worst of the weather and that the film would not show the full magnitude of the high seas and swell. The arbitrators were also impressed by the oral evidence from the Master of the vessel who they found an honest and reliable witness, corroborating evidence from another vessel in the area during the same time as the subject vessel, the extent of damage suffered by the vessel and the carrying away of the drums of lubricant.

Before the owners could invoke the perils of the sea defence they had to demonstrate that they had exercised due diligence to make the vessel seaworthy before the voyage commenced. The owners submitted evidence of the maintenance of the vessel prior to the voyage as well as contemporaneous evidence demonstrating the condition of the hatch covers.

The vessel had been in dry-dock one month prior to the voyage and had undergone general repairs including repairs to the hatch coamings. At this time hatchways and closing appliances were inspected by class surveyors and were found to be in good condition. A letter from the classification society stated that hose testing of the hatch covers was carried out with satisfactory results and that the surveyor was satisfied with the water tightness of the hatch covers. The Master had stated during his testimony before the arbitrators that the surveyor had not only watched the hose testing on the hatch covers, but also went down into each hatch after the test in order to ensure that there were no leakages. A ballast voyage was then undertaken between the dry-dock port and the first load port on the chartered voyage.

The owners also submitted contemporaneous evidence. The reports of three independent surveyors, who examined the hatch covers at the discharge port, confirmed their good order and condition. In addition, the surveyors' reports showed that there was salt water damage to all the hatches. If there had been salt water damage to only some of the hatches, the arbitrators may have drawn adverse inferences about the seaworthiness of these hatches. Finally, the video film taken by the Master demonstrated that the vessel on the whole looked well maintained and the hatch covers, in particular, appeared to be in good condition.

The arbitrators found that the evidence suggested that the owners had exercised due diligence to make the vessel seaworthy before the vessel sailed from the first load port. They also commented that they had no reason to believe that the hatch covers were not properly secured on the completion of loading.

The arbitrators further stated that in certain circumstances well maintained hatch covers will flex in periods of severe weather and permit the ingress of sea water. Therefore, provided owners had exercised due diligence to make the vessel seaworthy, they could avoid liability by relying on the perils of the sea defence.

Although it is very difficult to rely on a heavy weather defence, the arbitrators in the present case were impressed by the well kept log book and the video film.

Although not every vessel will have a video camera on board, a series of still photographs could also be of great evidential value in demonstrating bad weather and the condition of the vessel.

Chapter Two

INSURANCE COVER AND DAMAGE OR FAILURE OF SHIP'S OWN EQUIPMENT

Introduction

Although there are no legal requirements to compel a shipowner to insure his vessel (provided his vessel is free of mortgage commitments), most owners trading today have various forms of insurance cover. Normally, a shipowner may recover any loss which he suffers if:

• The damage is due to an insured peril

• The owner can provide sufficient evidence of the cause and extent of the damage suffered

• The vessel was in a seaworthy condition at the time of the incident which caused the loss and was engaged in a lawful trade, and

• The value of the loss exceeds any deductible/excess that may apply to the policy.

The legal requirement to demonstrate that the vessel was seaworthy effectively means that an owner has to be able to prove that, for the particular trade in which the vessel is involved, her hull, machinery and equipment are properly maintained, and that there are on board, sufficient stores, provisions, bunkers etc.

Accordingly, any damage to, failure of, or loss of these items which could affect the vessel's seaworthiness or the efficient state of the vessel must be reported to owners as soon as it occurs. This rule applies to any defect in the vessel which can be reasonably detected by the due diligence of the officers on board in the performance of their duties.

Owners are also under an obligation to maintain a safe working environment at all times on board the vessel. A relatively minor defect in a particular piece of equipment may affect the safety of the working environment. For example, a piece of machinery may have a safety feature which either becomes inoperative or detached (eg a defective foot operated emergency stop or a missing safety guard), and it then can become normal for the crew to operate it in this dangerous condition. The Master and the Safety Officer, therefore, must be constantly vigilant against such minor defects and must also ensure that the officers and crew use the safety equipment provided.

If the ship's equipment becomes damaged, owners will generally be able to recover any loss if the requirements listed above are fulfilled. However, the Master is under a duty to Underwriters to act as if the vessel is uninsured. Amongst other things, this means that, following damage, the owners' duty to Underwriters requires the Master, officers and crew to take such further measures as may be reasonable for the purpose of preventing or minimising losses covered by the Hull policy. The owners will be able to recover from Underwriters the costs of such measures as "sue and labour" expenses. He must also provide a full and complete record of the incident. This chapter examines the following:

To whom evidence should be given and the types of evidence required from the Master in the event of equipment failure -

Evidence relating to the cause of damage
Evidence required if damage causes stoppage or delay
Evidence required when damage or failure impairs vessel's efficiency

The scope of the insurance cover -

Risks covered -
Hull & Machinery
P&I
Roles of various parties involved -
Salvage Association
P&I Surveyor
Classification Society Surveyor

Stevedore damage
Charterparty clauses relating to stevedore damage are discussed.

Appendix
A case history is provided as an appendix to this chapter.

To whom evidence should be given

The Master and officers should always check, if necessary with owners, the credentials of anyone asking for evidence or attending for survey before giving evidence themselves or allowing crew to do so. Occasionally surveyors and lawyers representing interests opposed to owners will attempt to obtain evidence either by not disclosing, or even concealing the identity of those for whom they are working.

Evidence required from the vessel

Although the list provided below is not exhaustive, it gives an indication of the type of evidence required by the various parties involved in the event of equipment failure.

Evidence related to cause of damage

• Damage report prepared by the Master or Chief Engineer

• Photographs of the damaged equipment in place and after removal

- Parts of the damaged equipment and other relevant items which should be retained for inspection including consumables, such as old seals and broken bolts, analysis of which is often critical in determining cause of damage

- Log books and maintenance records relating to damaged equipment

- Any other records relating to the damaged equipment showing running hours, or evidence of previous inspections or surveys

- Reports from other personnel involved in the incident.

Evidence required if damage causes stoppage or delay (in addition to above)

- Deck and engine log books covering the period of the incident

- Statement of fuel remaining on board at the beginning and end of the stoppage

- Details of any deviation caused by the incident

- If deviation to a port of refuge is required:
  reports or confirmation of class by classification society surveyor
  statement of facts from port agent
  details of all shore assistance provided that it is attributable to damage

- Names of all the surveyors who have attended the vessel with full details of the organisations they represent

- Copies of fax, telex and radio messages sent or received, particularly those directed to time charterers dealing with deviation and off-hire times.

Evidence required when damage or failure impairs vessel's efficiency

- Details of additional time and fuel used as a consequence of the inefficiency

- Details of the extra labour and equipment used and a record of times when they were used

- Copies of all correspondence from the port agent, charterer or other third party holding vessel liable for delays.

In addition, the Master should:

Ensure that statements and time sheets are accurate before signing them

Ensure that written permission is obtained from the port authority if, as a result of delay caused by the vessel's inefficiency, the vessel has remained alongside a berth after completion of cargo operations. Many disputes have occurred when ships have remained alongside on the strength of the verbal assurance from jetty foreman, and consequently, owners have been faced with high penalty charges for remaining on the berth. The port agency will have details of charges involved.

Risks covered

The extent of cover provided by marine insurance policies varies enormously. The Master should verify his owner's cover for each vessel. The lists provided below give an indication of the type of risks covered by hull and machinery and protecting and indemnity ("P&I") policies.

Hull and Machinery (this list is compiled from the standard "ITC" clauses relating to damage to ship which were last revised on 01.11.95)

- Perils of the sea, rivers, lakes, or other navigable waters
- Fire, explosion
- Violent theft by persons outside the vessel
- Jettison
- Piracy
- Contact with land conveyance, dock or harbour equipment or installation
- Earthquake, volcanic eruption, or lightning
- Accidents in loading, discharging or shifting cargo or fuel
- Bursting of boilers, breakage of shafts, or any latent defect in the machinery or hull
- Negligence of the Master, officers, crew or pilots
- Negligence of repairers or charterers
- Barratry of Master, officers or crew
- Contact with aircraft, helicopters or similar objects, or objects falling therefrom.
- Pollution hazards (which includes damage to ship caused by preventive measures)
- Three-fourths collision liability (payment to third party).

P&I Cover (relating to damage to or failure of ship's equipment)

- Damage to third party's equipment and property
- One-fourth collision liability
- Oil pollution

Role of parties involved

Salvage Association - acting on behalf of hull underwriters

When damage to a vessel occurs which may give rise to a claim, owners have a duty to advise underwriters promptly. The underwriters will contact damage surveyors, usually the Salvage Association, who will in turn arrange for a surveyor to attend the vessel. The surveyor's job is to establish the facts surrounding the damage. The Salvage Association is an independent organisation which has representatives all over the world. In recent years, it has become common for Hull Underwriters to instruct the Salvage Association (or other independent surveyors) at an earlier stage to carry out comprehensive inspections of a vessel ("a condition survey") as a pre-condition of Underwriters agreeing to provide insurance for that vessel.

P&I surveyor - acting on behalf of owners

When damage occurs to the property of a third party - for example, if a pipe fails during bunkering and oil is spilled in to the harbour - owners' P&I Club will protect their interests in the ensuing investigation and clean up operation. When damage occurs, the owners or Master should alert the local P&I representative, who will instruct a surveyor to attend and assist. He will submit his report to the owners, and, if necessary, will also arrange security with the Club.

Classification Society Surveyor - acting on behalf of Class

- The role of a classification society in the merchant shipping community of today is to:

- Develop rules and standards for the design and construction of vessels

- Conduct surveys during the construction of vessels in order to verify that all rules and standards are complied with and to conduct regular surveys during a vessel's service in order to monitor the standard of maintenance

- Assign class when rules and standards are upheld.

When damage to any part of the ship occurs which could affect the vessel's seaworthiness, a surveyor representing the vessel's classification society will attend. All marine insurance policies impose an obligation on owners to maintain the vessel in class. If class is suspended as a result of a failure to comply with survey requirements or as a result of unrepaired damage, insurance cover is terminated automatically from that time. However, if the damage is an insured risk, termination of cover will only occur if the vessel sails from her next port of call without the prior approval of the classification society.

Stevedore damage

If stevedores cause damage to the ship's equipment, the Master must take care to comply with the terms of the charterparty relating to stevedores. Stevedores often are appointed by charterers, shippers or receivers. However, charterparties may contain terms which provide that charterers are not responsible for any damage caused by stevedores. Such clauses often provide:

- That the Master must notify stevedores of damages, normally by a written notice, within a very short time, usually 24 hours; the intention being that stevedores should have the opportunity to commission and pay for repairs before the vessel sails

- And that failing such notification, charterers, shippers, receivers and stevedores are to have no liability to owners.

Charterers, shippers, receivers and stevedores may not always escape liability as a result of such clauses. However, it is important that, insofar as possible the Master complies with any such clauses. Owner's position will always be assisted if the Master can obtain the stevedores' confirmatory signature to a description of the damage. Moreover, if all the documentation covering the incident has not been completed at the time of the incident, recovery may not be possible.

The Master should also ensure that all unrepaired stevedore damage is noted and photographed in detail in any off-hire survey and that charterers are invited to inspect damage repairs being carried out in dry-dock. If the damage is minor and does not effect the vessel's seaworthiness or efficient state, repairs may be deferred to the next dry-dock. Detailed reports by the Master and Chief Engineer of stevedore (and other types) of damage are invaluable not only as evidence for legal purposes, but also to owners in preparing comprehensive specifications before placing repair contracts and thus avoiding costs and delay which result when "Extras" are found to be necessary in the course of repairs.

Appendix 2:1

CASE HISTORY

The subject vessel was a chemical tanker, on passage from Swansea to Gothenburg and Fredericia. She was loaded with 990 MT of enthanol and isopropanol. She sailed from Swansea on 12 December, 1981.

On 13 December, the vessel met severe heavy weather with winds up to force 10. During the morning of 14 December, the wind increased to force 11. The vessel passed through the Dover Straits, and at 0648 hours, the Sandettie NE buoy was seen close on the starboard bow. The vessel's helm was put immediately hard over to port, but this failed to have any effect on her set. At 0650 hours, a bump was felt on her starboard quarter followed by an explosion and abnormal noises from the engine room.

It was assumed that the propeller had touched the chain of the buoy. The 2nd engineer, on duty in the engine room, promptly advised that the main engine gear box was vibrating and that smoke was issuing from the stern gland. He requested that the engine be stopped.

On stopping the main engine, an inspection was made of the main engine gear box, and it was observed that the gearbox casing had been completely fractured just above the holding down bolts. It was also noted that the propeller was being turned by water movement. In addition an inspection was made of the stern tube seals. These appeared to be intact as there was no evidence of leakage into the engine room.

A mayday call was sent by radio at 0655 hours requesting immediate tug assistance. The call was answered by the Dover and French coastguards, and another vessel in the vicinity agreed to stand by until a suitable tug arrived.

Attempts were made by the ship's engineers to secure the shafting, but these were unsuccessful due to heavy seas turning the propeller. A constant watch was kept on the vessel's position. Due to the strong WSW wind causing the vessel to drift towards Fairy Bank and the anticipated change in the current direction, the Master decided to anchor. At 0750 hours the port anchor was let go with the Fairy Bank buoy bearing 105 degrees, at a distance of two miles.

The vessel made radio contact with a tug steaming from Dunkirk at 1100 hours. The Master of the tug requested agreement of the service being rendered under Lloyd's Open Form of salvage agreement. This was accepted by the Master, and the tug came alongside at 1105 hours, at which time the standby vessel was released.

The Master explained to the tug Master that prior to commencement of tow, the vessel's propeller shaft would need to be secured to avert the possibility of the propeller turning (due to movement through the water), and causing failure of the stern tube seals. To assist this operation, the tug Master was requested to hold the vessel's head to windward. Connection of the tow was completed at 1227 hours, and by 1235 hours, the tug had hauled the vessel's head to windward. The ship's arrangement which secured the propeller shaft and gear box using timber, wires and bottle screws.

This work was completed by 1740 hours when the port anchor was weighed, and towage towards Dunkirk commenced. The vessel arrived in berth at Dunkirk at 2400 hours, following which the tug Master boarded, and the redelivery certificate was signed by the Master.

The following morning, the Master attended the offices of the tug owners and signed Lloyd's Open form of salvage agreement. Security was lodged by the owners with Lloyd's (£220,390 for the ship and freight and £29,610 for cargo).

On 15 December, a surveyor, appointed on behalf of hull underwriters, accompanied by another surveyor, acting on behalf of the classification society, and owners' superintendent, made an examination of the damage to the M.E. gear box. A diver was employed to inspect the vessel's bottom and stern area. The diver's report showed that two blades of the four bladed propeller were damaged, one of them damaged severely.

It now became apparent that the vessel's cargo would need to be discharged before the vessel could be repaired. As Dunkirk had no facilities for storage of the alcohol, it would become necessary to tow the vessel to a suitable port. Enquiries revealed that there were alcohol storage tanks available in Antwerp. A contract was arranged with the owners of the salvage tug for towage to Antwerp.

The classification surveyor agreed to permit towage, provided that the propeller shaft and gear box were secured in order to prevent the propeller turning during towage. The work was completed on 16 December, and the vessel left Dunkirk at 1145 hours under tow of the attending tug.

The tow was handed over to Antwerp tugs at the entrance to the river Scheldt, and the tow continued to Antwerp where the vessel berthed alongside the shore tank installations at 1118 hours on 17 December. Discharge of the cargo into the shore tanks was commenced at 1625 hours, and completed by 0305 hours on the 18 December. At this stage, gas freeing of the vessel's cargo tanks began.

At Dunkirk, a specification for repair of damage was drawn up, and two repair contractors in Antwerp and Hamburg were requested to submit repair quotations.

On the basis of these quotations, the repair contract was awarded to an Antwerp yard.

The vessel dry-docked following completion of gas freeing on 18 December. She was attended by the hull underwriters' surveyor and owners' superintendent. On examination it was found that the intermediate gear box casing, lower gear box casing, and the forward bearing housing were fractured. In addition, the gear teeth on both the pinion and main gear wheels were chipped and hammered, the flexible coupling was damaged, the intermediate shaft bearing brasses were fractured and distorted, three propeller blades were damaged to varying degrees, the tailshaft was bent, and finally, the tail shaft coupling bolts were damaged.

In view of the extensive damage, the gear box needed to be replaced. Enquiries revealed that a suitable gear box was not immediately available. The manufacturers of the original gear box agreed to deliver a new gear box by the end of March, 1982. The damaged gear box and coupling were removed from the vessel on the 23

41

December and delivered to the gear box manufacturers in order that some of the undamaged parts could be used in the new gear box.

The vessel remained in dry-dock until 29 January during which time all repairs apart from the work connected with the gear box and flexible coupling were undertaken. She was then placed alongside a lay-by berth awaiting arrival of the new gear box.

In view of the anticipated delay to the vessel, arrangements were made to charter a substitute vessel for delivery of the cargo to its destination. Loading of the cargo into the substitute vessel was carried out on 8 January. The cargo was delivered at Gothenburg on 11 January and at Fredericia on 12 January.

The new gear box and repaired flexible coupling were delivered to the yard on 27 March and fitted into the engine room. Installation of the gear box and realignment of the main engine were completed on 8 April. Following satisfactory engine trials and class approval, the vessel left Antwerp at 1648 hours the same day.

Under the terms of the Lloyd's Open Form of salvage agreement, negotiations were subsequently opened between various lawyers representing the ship and freight, cargo, and the tug owners. The parties agreed to salvage settlement of £100,000 plus the costs of the salvors' lawyers of £2,918.57. This amount of £102,918.57 was apportioned between ship and freight and cargo on the basis of the value adopted during negotiations, and the relative amounts were settled by the respective parties.

Main items of evidence used in claim

(Lloyd's standard form of Salvage agreement was signed by the Master on the owner's behalf on 15 December in Dunkirk).

Provided by the ship

- Deck log book

- Engine log book

- Master's report to the company

- Master's statement taken by the solicitor representing owners

- Chief engineer's statement taken by solicitor representing owners.

Provided by other sources

- Diver's report at Dunkirk

- Salvage Association's reports from surveyors at Dunkirk and Antwerp

- Class surveyor's report and certificate of seaworthiness for voyage to Antwerp

- Survey report covering transfer of cargo from ship to shore tanks in Antwerp

- Accounts and time sheets for all stages of investigation and repair

- Valuation certificate for vessel and cargo based on value at time of casualty

- General average adjustment.

Chapter Three

UNDER PERFORMANCE & OVER-CONSUMPTION CLAIMS

Introduction

Time charterparties usually describe a vessel as being capable of steaming fully laden, under good weather conditions, at about "x" knots on a consumption of about "y" tonnes of fuel oil and "z" tonnes of diesel oil. At the commencement of the charterparty the owners are required to ensure that the vessel is capable of performing in accordance with this description. Furthermore, commonly throughout the period of the charterparty the vessel will be required to maintain the warranted level of performance.

This chapter examines the following:

Evidence required from the vessel in under-performance or over-consumption claims:

• Speed

• Fuel consumption

• Basic information checklist

• Factors effecting performance

Speed and consumption of fuel

Claims, by time charterers for alleged under-performance of a vessel are commonly brought at the conclusion of a charterparty period. Under-performance claims in respect of speed usually go hand in hand with claims for "over-consumption of fuel". Defence of such claims requires accurate and comprehensive data to be collected by the vessel. This evidence must be detailed and comprehensive and the responsibility for collecting such evidence falls largely to the Master, chief engineer and his officers.

Speed

The first point of reference for the determination of a vessel's performance should be the charterparty. The charterparty will often provide a detailed method of assessment of a vessel's performance. Where no specific method of assessment is given in the charterparty a vessel's performance is assessed in good weather conditions (commonly Beaufort force 4 or less - unless otherwise described in the charterparty). The vessel's performance in good weather periods should be calculated. The good weather speed is then simply extrapolated and applied to the whole duration of the charterparty, when compared with the warranted charterparty speed, any time lost (or saved) can be determined.

Whilst the vessel's deck log book will often contain most of the basic details required in order to perform the necessary calculations, further information may be of considerable assistance. Details of any factors reducing the vessel's performance should be noted (either in the deck log or movement book, including engine room log book and chief engineer's log/fuel extracts). For example, alterations of course for traffic avoidance purposes, periods of slow steaming, stoppages, engine/machinery breakdown, adverse tidal streams and currents experienced should all be noted.

Accurate details of the weather conditions experienced should be noted in the vessel's deck log book. In addition independent verification of the weather conditions can be of assistance in avoiding disputes as to the extent of any "good weather periods", in this regard copies of all weather reports received by the vessel should be retained.

Consumption of fuel

In addition to the weather records contained within the deck log books and independent weather forecasts etc. details of the fuel consumed by the vessel whilst on passage should be retained. In addition careful records of all periods when the vessel is instructed to proceed at an economical speed or when the vessel is navigating in congested waters and using diesel oil should be made.

It is of vital importance that an accurate record of fuel consumption is maintained, both for main engines, boilers and auxiliaries. On watch keeping vessels fuel flow meter readings should be recorded on a watch by watch basis whilst on UMS ships this should be recorded at least daily, usually at noon. When changing over fuel, if applicable, for manoeuvring all flow meter readings should be updated.

Check list

The following items are essential in collecting sufficient evidence to properly defend a speed/consumption claim.

Whenever possible this information must be collected contemporaneously and recorded on a daily basis.

• Direction of wind and sea

• Beaufort wind force

• Swell

• Direction of swell

• Height and length of waves

• Propeller - rpm

• Noon position

- Observed and actual from accurate position fixing device is fitted
- Log speed
- Air and sea temperature
- Barometric pressure
- Vessel's course
- Fuel flow meter readings
- Fuel tank soundings
- Periods when vessel full away on passage
- Periods when manoeuvring - when change over fuels if applicable
- Periods of increased fuel consumption:
  - air conditioning
  - high electrical load
  - tank cleaning
  - incinerators, etc.
- Alterations of course
- Reduction in speed:
  - charterer's instruction - slow steaming
  - owner's instruction
  - weather conditions
  - machinery factors/failure, etc.
  - change of ballast
- Prevailing currents
- Deck log books
- Engine log books
- Oil record books - purification, transfer etc.
- Fuel loading, handling, consumption records (C/E Extracts).

Chapter Four

BUNKER DISPUTES

Introduction

In recent years there has been a general deterioration in the quality of fuel supplied for bunkers. Sub-standard fuel is one major cause of loss of speed and over-consumption of fuel and may also have a detrimental effect on the vessel's machinery. The Master should take care to ensure that the bunkers supplied match the specifications required by the vessel. If poor quality fuel has been supplied, the Master should follow the correct procedures, which are listed below, in order to minimise damage. In case the fuel does cause engine damage and any subsequent expense and loss of time, it is important that the Master records all the relevant information listed below in order to establish the cause of the damage, particular attention being given to the retention and preservation of samples. Finally, in addition to thorough reporting procedures, the Master should promptly report the matter to owners.

Procedure at commencement of bunkering - all of which should be suitably documented or recorded:

- The chief engineer should be responsible for supervising bunkering and should liaise closely with the officer of the watch. Company bunkering procedures should be strictly adhered to and all safety and anti-pollution measures must be fully considered.

- The flash point, viscosity and other characteristics of fuel supplied should be checked to ensure that the fuel is suitable for the vessel for on board combustion. Particular care should be taken, with the use of very heavy fuel oils, to ensure the vessel's fuel heating capacity is sufficient to enable efficient combustion of any bunkers loaded.

  If the fuel fails to confirm with the specifications required by the vessel, the Master should notify in writing the bunker supplier and charterers' port agents (sample letters which should be sent to bunker supplier and charterers' port agents are provided at pages 49 to 52)

- The chief engineer, barge master/shoreman should check the security of the hose couplings on the bunker barge and on the receiving vessel, take appropriate anti-pollution precautions and should agree start up, topping off and bunkering rates. A clear system of communications must be established between barge/shore and ship. Emergency shut down signals must be confirmed

  Failure to observe these precautions may lead to oil pollution and result in heavy fines and possibly even the arrest of the vessel

- **Sound** all **tanks** on board the vessel and the bunker barge, where the supply is by barge and where this is possible, before taking bunkers and on completion of bunkering and record all soundings. Where bunkers are loaded from shore, whenever possible, shore readings should be confirmed including flow meter readings and tank sounds

- New bunkers should be segregated from old bunkers on board. If bunkers are mixed, a mixed sample of the old and new fuels must be tested for compatibility. An additional sample should be retained on board the vessel

- New bunkers should be tested regularly for the presence of water after loading. To do so it should be ensured that the vessel is well provided with a good quality water finding preparation. The on board treatment of fuel oil is vital, particularly centrifuging. The results should then be checked against engine manufacturer's specifications

- Normal representative samples taken, for example, by continuous drip during bunkering, which should be marked and sealed, should be taken at the vessel's manifold and the |Master should request in writing the supplier or charterers' port agents to attend during sampling (the sample letter is provided in Sample 3). Only special sample containers should be used and it must be ensured that these are scrupulously clean before use.

  If the suppliers or port agents fail to attend, the Master must make a protest in writing (a sample letter is provided in Appendix 4:1).

  One sample should be sent for analysis immediately. If possible the bunkers should not be used until the results are available.

  The use of reputable fuel analyses laboratories is strongly recommended, some major analysis programmes can supply very prompt results. It may also be appropriate to consider appointing a duly qualified independent surveyor to carry out or oversee the taking of bunker samples.

- Often the ship will be presented with samples by the supplier. If possible, try to attend that sampling and record the details of where and when it was carried out, by whom, by what method, and who was in attendance.

Procedure if it is suspected that sub-standard bunkers have been placed on board

- Records must be kept of which tanks the bunkers were placed on delivery and whether or not there was oil in the tanks prior to delivery and if so, full details must be given, including the specification of those bunkers, where and when they were supplied, how much and by whom

- The location of the tank in which the suspect bunkers had been kept must be recorded and full details of all movements of bunkers between tanks must be noted

- Details of ullages must be noted and copies of bunker receipts for the new bunkers must be preserved together with copies of bunker receipts for the most recent previous bunkerings

- All notes of protest and the engine and deck logs must be preserved

- At least one sealed sample taken during bunkering must be retained and samples from previous bunkers kept safe on board until specific instructions received from owners to dispose of the samples

- A note must be kept of the following:
  - The chief engineer and other crew members involved in the bunkering operation
  - The names of those present at the time the bunker samples were taken
  - The crew members involved in correcting any problems associated with sub-standard bunkers

- Owners must be notified promptly.

Procedures if sub-standard bunkers are used and damage results:

- In addition to the information referred to above, the Master should also keep records of the following:
  - When was fuel first burned
  - What were the immediate manifestations of the problem
  - What action was taken to reduce the problem
  - Was the action effective
  - When were repairs carried out and under whose supervision
  - What parts were overhauled or renewed
  - When was contaminated fuel last burnt
  - Disposition of contaminated fuel
  - Performance of engine once the vessel had ceased to burn contaminated fuel
  - Any additives that may have been used in the fuel, the quantities used, how and when they were added and into which tanks
  - How the particular batch of fuel in question was treated on board prior to use, for example how separators and filters were used

- If available, all contemporaneous reports of repairs from owners, charterers, engine manufacturers and underwriters' surveyors should be kept

- Any damaged machinery parts should be kept for future inspection

- Photographs should be taken of damaged parts when discovered.

Appendix 4:1

Notification by Master to charterers' port agents and bunker supplier that supplied fuel does not conform with specifications required by the vessel.

FROM:
COMPANY:

TO: DATE:
                                                            TIME:
                                                            AT:

Re: MV
Bunkers loaded at

I hereby give you notice that an analysis carried out on this vessel of a representative sample of the bunkers supplied by you indicates the deficiencies listed below. The fuel is therefore outside the specification of fuel suitable to the vessel's engines and auxiliary machinery and has been submitted for further analysis.

Deficiencies were noted in:

1 Density   [ ]
2 Viscosity   [ ]
3 Pour point   [ ]
4 Water content   [ ]
5 Salt water   [ ]
6 Compatibility   [ ]
7 Catalytic fines   [ ]

Owners await charterers' instructions and until these are received, the vessel cannot proceed. In the meantime, the vessel's engineering staff will use their best endeavours to protect the vessel's engines (including the slowing and stopping of the ship's machinery when necessary). Owners hold charterers fully responsible for any damage, delays, poor performance, over-consumption or any other loss or expense arising as a direct or indirect consequence of your failure to supply suitable fuel.

Yours faithfully
Master

Make and model of sampling equipment:
Make and model of main engine:

Notification by Master to charterers' port agents and bunker supplier that fuel supplied does not conform with specification required by the vessel and is unusable.

FROM:
COMPANY:

TO: DATE:
                                                                             TIME:
                                                                             AT:

Re: MV
Bunkers loaded at

I hereby give you notice that a shipboard analysis of a representative sample of the bunkers supplied by you to the vessel indicates that the fuel is wholly unsuitable for use in the vessel's machinery.

In the circumstances, I cannot jeopardise the safety of the vessel, crew, or cargo by accepting or using the bunkers supplied without first receiving express instructions to do so from you and owners.

In the meantime, owners hold charterers wholly responsible for all damages and delays and other loss and expense arising as a direct or indirect consequence from your failure to supply suitable fuel.

Yours faithfully

Master

Make and model of sampling equipment:
Make and model of main engine:

Request from Master to charterers' port agents and bunker supplier to attend during representative sampling.

FROM:
COMPANY:

TO: DATE:
                                                       TIME:
                                                       AT:

Re: MV
Samples of bunkers

[In accordance with charterparty conditions] I hereby request you to ensure that representative samples of the bunkers to be supplied to the vessel will be taken and sealed in the presence of competent and authorised representatives of charterers and the vessel, such samples to be taken during bunkering at the vessel's manifold. The vessel will require two samples.

It will be of assistance to you to know that the vessel has facility for drawing continuous samples at the manifold. If no joint samples are taken during bunkering by a satisfactory alternative system, only those samples drawn at the manifold by the vessel's representatives will be regarded as representative samples.

I shall be grateful if you will advise me as soon as possible what arrangements have been made by you or the bunker supplier in respect of bunkering and sampling.

Yours faithfully

Master

Vessel's authorised personnel:
Make and model of sampling equipment:
Make and model of main engine:

Protest by Master for failure of charterers' port agents or bunker supplier to attend during representative sampling.

FROM:
COMPANY:

TO: DATE:
                                                                         TIME:
                                                                         AT:

Re: MV
Samples of bunkers

I hereby make a formal protest that you and the bunker supplier have failed to participate in the proper obtaining and sealing during bunkering time of representative samples of the bunkers supplied to the vessel.

In particular:

   No samples have been drawn by you and supplied   [ ]
   Ready sealed samples have been supplied   [ ]
   Samples were drawn in a method which is unsatisfactory
   and susceptible to gross error   [ ]

I hereby give you notice that the vessel has taken her own samples during the bunkering operation [which were sealed in the presence of charterers or bunker supplier's representative] [in the absence of a response to my invitation to attend joint sampling] and only these samples will be regarded as representative. Two sealed samples drawn by the vessel are available to you on request.

Yours faithfully

Master

Make and model of sampling equipment:
Make and model of main engine:

Chapter Five

UNSAFE PORTS AND BERTHS

Introduction

Charterparties often provide that a port or berth is "safe". This means the charterers must nominate a port which at the relevant time the particular ship may approach, use, and depart from without - in the absence of some abnormal occurrence - being exposed to danger which cannot be avoided by good seamanship and navigation.

Charterers obligations
Time charters

Where time charters have the option to nominate a safe port within a specified range, the obligation to nominate a **safe port** arises at the time when the order is given, so they must nominate a port which is then expected to be safe for the ship to approach, use, and leave.

If the port later becomes unsafe, charterers must issue new orders - if necessary to proceed to another port. However, this obligation does not arise in a case where the port later becomes unsafe due to an unexpected and abnormal danger which the charterers were unaware.

If charterers nominate a port which, in the Master's opinion is unsafe, he should immediately contact his owners explaining in detail the reasons for his opinion and request further instructions. If the Master reasonably obeys the charterer's orders to proceed to the port and the ship becomes damaged as a result, charterers will be liable; he must, however, act reasonably. If, for example, the weather deteriorates and the ship faces ranging damage if she stays on the berth the Master should depart from the berth if he can do so safely; if he remains on the berth the damage arising will not automatically fall on the charterers even though the berth is an unsafe one.

It is important the Master considers carefully voyage orders given by the charterers before proceeding to a port and follows closely any instructions given by the charterers.

Voyage charters

Voyage charterers must nominate, from the range of ports specified within the charterparty, a safe port. However, it is uncertain whether the secondary obligation to issue new orders for another safe port arises in the case of voyage charters. Where a port is specifically named in a voyage charter it is up to the owners to establish that the port is safe before fixing, unless the charterers have stated that it is safe.

Oil charters

Oil charters often provide that the charterers only have to exercise due diligence to select a safe port. The charterers' obligations are clearly more limited in this case.

Elements of safety
Port must be safe to approach and leave

Charterers must nominate a port which the ship can both safely approach and depart from. If the berth is upriver the river passage must be safe. Although charterers are not under an obligation to ensure that the most direct route or any particular route to or from the port (or berth) is safe, they must ensure that the voyage they order is one that an ordinarily prudent and skilful Master can make safely.

The particular ship

The port must be safe for the particular ship at the relevant time. The fact that ships of a different size or characteristics or differently laden, could have safely used the port is irrelevant. A port will be unsafe if the ship cannot approach it without dismantling part of her structure, or if the ship has to discharge part of her cargo into lighters if her draft is too great for the port. However, "safe" does not mean "without delay". So a bar harbour will not be unsafe simply because a ship cannot use it without delay at all times and tides.

Port must be safe to use

The location, layout and other physical characteristics of a nominated port must be safe for the ship. A structured and integrated arrangement of "port systems" as required by the ship should be provided by a port, ie:

- Available port information, charting, etc.

- Navigation aids, lights, buoys, etc.

- Pilotage service

- Tugs

- Berth protection, fendering

- Mooring facilities

- Weather service

- Communications.

A port will not be unsafe because the vessel has to leave in certain weather conditions, provided the onset of these conditions are predictable and the Master has been given adequate warning to leave or been made aware that he should keep watch for local warnings. The port must also have an adequate system to warn of approaching danger and an adequate weather forecasting system, a sufficient number of pilots and tugs available, and an adequate system for ensuring that there is always searoom and room to manoeuvre.

Good navigation and seamanship

A port will not be unsafe if any dangers inherent in it may be avoided by good navigation and seamanship. The Master is under a duty to take whatever reasonable steps are necessary to avoid or reduce these dangers.

If, for example, the weather deteriorates and the ship faces ranging damage if she stays on the berth the Master should depart from the berth if he can do so safely; if he remains on the berth the damage arising will not automatically fall on the charterers even though the berth is an unsafe one.

However, if the dangers may be overcome only by exercising extraordinary standards of navigation and seamanship, the port will be considered unsafe.

The shipowner is usually responsible for the Pilot's errors or omissions in navigation and shiphandling; and also for the utilisation and disposition of port tugs provided under a standard towage contract. The owners can only avoid this responsibility if they can show the pilotage or tug "system" at the port to be defective as a whole; so that Pilots are, for example, habitually ill-trained, incompetent or drunk, or are provided with inadequate hydrographic or other information to do a competent job and advise the Master accurately on port matters.

VTS (Vessel Traffic Service) information should never be regarded as pilotage information or advice; the law concerning pilotage is unambiguous inasmuch as the conning of the vessel may only be undertaken from the wheelhouse or within the vicinity of the ship.

Abnormal occurrences

A port will not be unsafe in the legal sense if the damage to the vessel occurred as a result of an abnormal occurrence, ie one not characteristic of the port. Abnormal occurrences are typically unexpected wars and ships stranding in the channel - not occurrences which arise out of the operation of the port systems.

Evidence required from the Mariner

When an accident involving an unsafe berth or port occurs, the information required to bring a claim against charterers may concern not only the facts of the incident, but relate back to matters as early as the port at which the voyage planning commenced.

To ensure that all relevant information required is available, the Master/mariner should consult the following checklists and maintain and retain relevant records.

Port CCTV and VHF recordings

It is worth bearing in mind that a great many ports employ CCTV (Close Circuit Television) and VHF (Very High Frequency Radio) recording facilities themselves, especially for critical areas of navigation (such as areas of restricted manoeuvrability, passage through lock systems, etc.). It is therefore important that the Master strives to obtain the fullest details for preparation of the vessel's defence or claim.

The approach voyage

Charterers' safe port promise also applies to any necessary route to or from the river, eg via a river. Details of up-to-date information supplied to river pilots by the pilotage or port authority should be requested and any refusal or inability on the part of the pilot to share such information should be noted in the deck log book.

General

- Complete record of communications dealing with the voyage and voyage orders

- Charts, plans of port, berth or anchorage

- General arrangement plans, mooring arrangement plan and other relevant ship's plans

- Deck, engine, radio logs, bell book, Chief Officer's cargo book

- Sketch of berth facilities

- Miscellaneous published information concerning port

- Note of protest

- Detailed records of all services supplied by third parties

- Printed record information, course recorder, engine movement, echo sounder, etc.

- A record of when bridge and engine clocks were synchronised

- All charts in use at the time of the incident (no alteration should be made) together with all rough notes and calculations from the chart table, including passage planning documentation

- All communications with third parties together with any hand-written notes of oral/VHF communications

- Third parties should be requested to issue reports of services provided to be verified by the Master.

Pilotage

If an accident occurs whilst the ship is under pilotage or awaiting a pilot for sailing, details should be sought concerning the following points, where appropriate:

- Names of pilots on duty

- Berthing procedures

- Call-out procedures

- Date of last hydrographic survey

- Names of other vessels in port and where berthed, together with traffic movements

- Name of person advising Pilot of ship's details and record of details given.

Tugs

- Tugs owners / authority / tugs names
- Number of units available
- Horsepower / bollard pull / propulsion
- Where stationed
- Call-out procedure
- Communication facilities / radio watch
- Duty roster / crew lists
- Operational limits.

Moorings

On-board:

- Sketch of mooring arrangements identifying station, material, size and security system
- Anti-chafe measures
- Mooring rope / wire details - invoices, test certificates, repairs, when first used
- Retain failed / damaged equipment as evidence
- Storage details
- Winch details
- Mooring watch details
- Damaged / parted rope / wire, where parted and how secured
- Number of lines onboard
- Mooring advice from Pilot, berthing Master, port authority, etc.
- Photographs, samples.

Ashore:

- Bollards - type, distance apart, etc.
- Mooring line lead
- Mooring gangs
- Mooring arrangements approval by port authority / terminal operator.

The berth

- Design / construction details

- Fender type - sketch or photograph

- Sketch or photograph of fender positions along ship's length

- Condition of fenders at time of berthing

- Advice from agent, pilot, port authority

- Communication with agent, etc. about missing or defective fenders

- Fender arrangements at adjacent berths - condition, disposition, etc.

- Ship's fenders

- Constraints at berth - water depth, position of other vessels, turning area, etc.

Weather services

In port:
Details of the following should be obtained:

- Port information booklet

- Port weather service

- Local radio

- Warnings provided by port authority to vessels and/or agents

- Any specific advice on arrival about local weather characteristics

- Storm signal - where sited?

- Record of all weather forecasts and weather fax charts.

On board:

- ALRS Volume 3 - Radio Weather Services (or similar publication)

- NP283a - Weather Reporting and Forecast Areas (or similar publication)

- Weather facsimile - working? performance? stations used?

- Radio officer's watch keeping schedule

- Radio log

- Log book or other record of weather, swell, barometric pressure, etc.

- Communications with port authority, agents, pilotage authority, other vessels, etc.

- Weather charts and messages received

- Anemometer - where sited?

Photographic evidence

The importance of contemporaneous photographic evidence cannot be over-emphasised. In order to assist the successful prosecution of an unsafe port claim, the officer should consider it part of his duties to arrange for a crew member to photograph the following during the approach stage and after coming alongside, as may be appropriate:

- Sea conditions at anchorage

- Strong currents in rivers, ice, and other hazards

- The berths fenders and condition of concrete apron

- Approaches to locks, condition of fendering for entry and within, if appropriate

- Condition of locks and evidence of any previous damage

- Mooring arrangements

- Areas of berth particularly exposed to swell

- Other vessels affected by adverse conditions

- Any lack of room to manoeuvre in port

- Fender arrangements at adjacent berths (for comparative purposes)

- Any damage to the ship or port installations.

CASE HISTORY - 1

The vessel involved in this incident was a 120,000 DWT bulk carrier which had been time chartered for a period of 11 to 13 months, charterer's option. The charterparty was on the New York Produce Exchange Form with the vessel to be employed carrying lawful merchandise between safe ports within institute warranty limits. The charterparty contained an arbitration clause whereby all disputes between owners and charterers were to be resolved by arbitration in London. In accordance with the terms of the charterparty, the charterers ordered the vessel to load a cargo of coal in Queensland for discharge at a nominated port in Japan.

The vessel arrived at the named port in December and commenced discharge on arrival. Weather conditions deteriorated, and northerly winds caused the vessel to range against the quay on a heavy swell. The stress generated on the fenders by the vessel's movement resulted in the disintegration and failure of one fender unit, which caused the fracture of the vessel's shell plating in a number of places. Further damage was then caused by contact with the unprotected section of wharf under continued pressure from the wind and swell.

As a consequence of this accident, owners incurred substantial off-hire and repair costs. Owners commenced arbitration proceedings in London to recover the loss from the charterer.

Owners claimed that the nominated port was unsafe for the following reasons:

• There was no protection from northerly winds in the port

• There was no system in operation at the port to provide protection at the berth or to enable the vessel to leave the berth quickly if weather conditions demanded such action

• There was no satisfactory system in operation at the port for providing warnings about deteriorating weather conditions

• The fenders on the wharf were inadequate for vessels of the size scheduled to use the facility. Additionally, the fenders were not properly equipped in that the chains required to limit the upward and downward movement of the fenders were missing on some units

• The berth was not provided with a system of mooring points which allowed balanced and effective use of mooring ropes and wires. This unbalanced mooring system resulted in bits being placed at other than optimum angles which exacerbated the movement of the vessel against the quay when under the influence of a strong northerly wind.

The arbitrators found that the charterer's were in breach of their contractual obligation to nominate a safe port for the following reasons:

• The berth was over-exposed to the elements. The breakwater afforded little reduction in the wind and swell conditions present at the time of the casualty

- No tugs were immediately available

- The construction of the berth was such that the facilities to moor did not enable the vessel to have a symmetrical mooring layout. The berth had been lengthened to accommodate two vessels, and as a result, the stern of the vessel overhung the end of the berth. There were no mooring posts on the berth for stern lines except a distant post on the shore. Therefore, the stern lines were some three times the length of the head lines. In bad weather conditions, the movement of the vessel caused excessive pressure on one fender as a result of which it collapsed into the water. Further movement brought the vessel into contact with the exposed concrete causing severe shell damage

- The fender which collapsed may not have been sufficiently strong.

The arbitrators rejected the charterer's arguments that the weather was exceptionally severe. They found that although weather conditions were unusual, they were not abnormally so. The arbitrators further rejected the charterer's arguments that the Master had been negligent in the mooring of the vessel and the lines had become slack. They held that the Master had acted in accordance with the standards of prudent seamanship.

CASE HISTORY - 2

This case history, also involving a bulk carrier, emphasises not only the obligations of the charterers, but also the duty of those onboard to exercise reasonable care.

The bulk carrier was lying alongside in a port subject on occasion, to heavy swell conditions and the likelihood of ranging at the berth.

The port "system" did not provide for warning moored vessels of the onset of deteriorating weather conditions or the likelihood of a dangerous swell in the inner harbour. There was no system which could forewarn the Master of the possible need to vacate the berth, and no information was passed to the vessel by either the port authority or ship's agents.

The sequence of events was as follows:

1000   Wind suddenly increased, RSBE, mooring lines continuously tended and further moorings set out

1030   Westerly wind blowing strong, both anchors dropped, ballast tanks filled, parted aft breast-line immediately replaced

1100   Westerly wind still blowing strong, heavy northerly swell entering inner harbour causing ship to range alongside quay, vessel rolling heavily, additional fendering placed but crushed due to ship's movement

1120   Gale force wind, rain and hail, For'd and after ropes continually parting but immediately replaced, vessel's violent movement alongside quay causing hull damage on contact

61

	with quay, main engine's used to assist in easing vessel's fore and aft motion
1230	Continuation of same weather conditions and vessel's heavy ranging against quay, request made through pilot station for tugs assistance to hold and secure vessel
1240	Contact established with pilot station
1310- 1316	Two tugs in attendance assisting vessel, but vessel continuing to strike quay
1330	Master requested agent (via landline telephone) for vessel to be shifted to another safer berth as present discharge berth totally unsafe
1400	Tugs depart, weather improves slightly allowing a visual inspection of considerable impact damage
1500	Agent onboard, and following discussion and contact with port authority, permission granted to shift. Harbour radio indicated weather forecast to deteriorate after nightfall
1600	Pilot onboard, three tugs in attendance, commenced singling-up
1830	Vessel secured to different berth.

The charterers alleged the Master was negligent in not leaving the berth as soon as the weather deteriorated, that is about 1000, rather than awaiting assistance from pilot and tugs. The Master's evidence indicated that by 1030 if he remained alongside, his vessel would suffer hull damage, indeed, he was inclined to this view as early as 1000.

Expert opinion suggested that if it was bad enough to drop both anchors then it was bad enough to vacate the berth.

The arbitrators took the view that the Master should not have left the berth immediately as to have done so without tug and pilot assistance would have placed the vessel in further danger. However, he should have decided to leave the berth at 1030 and ordered tugs and pilot then. He did not do this and therefore failed to exercise reasonable care and skill at that time.

Since the significant damage commenced at 1100, the arbitrators judged the charterers liable for damage between 1100 and 1130, and the shipowner liable for damage thereafter because of the Master's actions.

The claim was apportioned in such a manner that owners had to pay 85% damage cost repairs, and charterers 15%.

Chapter Six

DAMAGE TO FIXED AND FLOATING OBJECTS

Introduction

Damage caused by a vessel to third party property, such as any harbour, dock, pier, quay, jetty, land or anything whatsoever fixed or movable (more commonly referred to as "fixed or floating objects"), can often give rise to large claims which owners have great difficulty defending. In many countries, owners will be strictly liable which means that the vessel will be responsible for any accidental damage, although the vessel and crew were in no way at fault. The damage may be caused by a vessel coming into direct contact with, for example, a dock, pier, jetty, buoy, or crane, or the damage may be caused by the vessel's wash. In most instances, claims for the damage caused by the vessel will be covered by the vessel's P&I insurance (the reader should refer to chapter 2 for a discussion on risks covered by insurance).

This chapter examines the following:

When incidents occur

Evidence required from the vessel.

In Appendix 6:1 two short case studies are provided.

When incidents occur

Damage to fixed and floating objects usually occur when a vessel is entering or leaving a port. If damage occurs when a vessel is entering a port, the Master should report the incident as soon as possible to owners. If possible, the Master also should contact the local P&I representatives and request them to attend and assist.

If damage occurs when the vessel is leaving a port, the Master should resist any temptation to ignore the incident in the hope that the damage will be minimal and there were no witnesses. Owners should be notified as soon as possible in order that enquiries may be made to ascertain the extent of the damage.

Occasions arise where a vessel has to moor to a fixed or floating object which has already suffered damage on one or more previous occasions and the damage remains extant. In such cases the master should draw the attention of the Port Authorities to this, and note the details of the damage in the log, and support this with sketches and photographic evidence.

It is not unknown for damage to be claimed against more than one vessel for the same alleged damage. These allegations are usually made when the vessel was **leaving** the berth.

Evidence required from the vessel

In cases of substantial damage, owners and their insurers will appoint expert surveyors and in some cases civil engineers, to assess the extent of any damage and repairs. In order to assist the surveyors, who may not arrive at the scene immediately, it is essential that the Master assembles as much contemporaneous evidence as possible. The manner in which Port Watches were routinely maintained would inevitably have a bearing on the value of such evidence.

However, the Master should note that it is not only major incidents which require vigilance. Minor contacts with fixed and floating objects can lead to substantial claims by local authorities. Unless the owners and their insurers are able to produce contemporaneous evidence from the vessel they will have considerable difficulty refuting the allegations and minimising the extent of any claim.

The Master should ensure that the report of the incident which he prepares includes the following information:

- The date, time, and location, of the incident -

  The information should be as precise as possible, for example, if the vessel comes into contact with a pier, the Master should note the number of the pier

- The conditions prevailing at the time -

  The Master should note whether it was day or night, the weather conditions, visibility, sea state, the incidence of swell, and the state of tides and currents

- Details of the vessel's manoeuvres -

  The Master should note whether the vessel was entering or leaving a port or locks, berthing, assisted by tugs, or whether there was a pilot on board the vessel

- Names and addresses of all crew members, pilots, tug crews, shore workers, or any other persons who witnessed the incident -

  If time allows, the Master should attempt to obtain from the witnesses their account of the incident

- Details of the damaged object -

  The Master should note whether the damaged object was old or new, whether it was well used, whether it was well illuminated and marked, whether there were any signs of damage or defects to the object other than that caused by the vessel. If possible, the Master should ensure that photographs, video recordings or sketches of the damage are taken.

An incident involving a fixed or floating object may also give rise to an unsafe port claim against charterers of the vessel. Therefore, the Master should refer to the discussion of unsafe ports and berths in chapter five for the type of evidence required from the vessel.

CASE HISTORY - 1

The subject vessel came into contact with a disused jetty in Wilhelmshaven, and the port authorities brought a claim for damages against the owners. The attending surveyors found that the jetty was not marked and, more importantly, not illuminated. The port authorities denied these allegations. However, the Master, shortly after the incident, had collected evidence from the crew that the jetty was not lit and made particular reference to this point in his report. This contemporaneous evidence which supported the surveyors' findings, persuaded the port authorities to substantially reduce their claim for damages.

CASE HISTORY - 2

A loaded tanker whilst approaching its berth allegedly made heavy contact with one of the fenders. The fender, of a compound rubber shock absorbing type, showed evidence of not only the new damage but of pre-existing damage and recent temporary repairs. Doppler radar was fitted to the berth and was said to have been in use at the time that the vessel arrived. The claimants failed to provide a recording of the doppler radar in support of their argument.

A P&I surveyor was invited to attend the casualty before the vessels departure and collated details regarding the displacement of the vessel, the mooring operation, use of tugs, speed and angle of approach to the berth. Accurate log books maintained on the bridge and engine room provided valuable corroborative evidence to indicate that the contact could not have occurred in the manner described by the terminal. This further enabled the owners and their P&I Club to demonstrate that the alleged damages could not have been solely attributed to the incident.

Owners contribution to the claim was properly limited to that amount which would have restored the fender to its condition immediately prior to the arrival of the vessel.

Chapter Seven

POLLUTION

Introduction

Pollution incidents on the scale of the *EXXON VALDEZ*, the *HAVEN*, and the *SEA EMPRESS* are rare. However, the resulting devastation to the environment and marine life has had such a far-reaching effect on international opinion that most countries will now deal severely with vessels which discharge even small quantities of pollutant within their territorial waters. It should be noted that pollution incidents may not necessarily be limited to discharges of oil as cargo or bunkers. Pollution may also emanate from non-tank vessels whether from cargo, bunkers, garbage or smoke emissions.

Vessels which pollute the environment are likely to be penalised whether or not the Master or crew are in any way to blame; this is often referred to as "strict liability" or "the polluter pays" principle. In instances where strict liability applies, it still remains possible for the shipowner to recover from other parties who are at fault in causing the incident; for example, from the owners of another vessel involved in a collision. In some jurisdictions, however, if it can be established that the pollution was not caused by the fault of the vessel and that all reasonable precautions were taken to minimise or prevent the pollution, fines or other penalties may be reduced or waived.

However, the extent to which other parties to the incident may be pursued and successful recoveries made, or establishing that reasonable steps were taken to minimise or prevent the pollution will depend upon the evidence which can be gathered at the time of the incident and immediately thereafter.

This chapter examines the following:

Sources of pollution

Precautions to minimise the risk of spills

Procedures to be followed in the event of a pollution incident

Evidence required from the vessel

International regulations

In Appendix 7:1, the international regulations dealing with pollution are discussed. Two studies are included in Appendix 7:2.

Sources of pollution

There are three main sources of pollution:

* Collision, fire, explosion or grounding

* Intentional discharge of oil, cargo residue, garbage or other waste from the vessel; for example, the pumping of bilges, or deballasting of cargo tanks

* Accidental pollution while transferring fuel, cargo, garbage or other waste to or from the vessel.

However, there is also an increasing tendency in some areas of the world to impose fines against the vessel for excessive smoke emission, and in some instances for excessive noise levels.

Precautions to minimise the risk of pollution
A. Oil/chemical spills

Procedures relating to oil/chemical transfers should form part of every vessels' standing instructions. Such procedures should also be followed during bunkering operations which are common to not only oil/product tankers, but also to all types of vessel. These procedures should include the name of a supervising officer who is in charge of transfer operations, and an outline of pipe-lines and valve operations. The procedures should also emphasise the necessity of cementing scuppers and save-all plugs in drip trays and the checking of moorings. They should also contain an outline of clean-up operations.

Owners, together with the Master, should ensure that a system of safe operation is installed on board the vessel to minimise the risk of oil/chemical spills. Such a system should include the following practices:

* Oil/chemical spill drills of the same type as boat drills, fire drills and emergency tank drills. All crew must be carefully trained in the use and application of appropriate dispersants/neutralising agents but it should be clearly pointed out that in any event, such dispersants/neutralising agents should not be used without the prior consent of the Master who in turn must check with the appropriate local authority that such use is permissible

* Careful disposal of ballast water which has been contaminated with oil/chemicals whether the vessel is at sea or within port limits

* Frequent inspections of the equipment used in cargo or bunkering operations, the times and results of which are noted in the appropriate log book. Oil spills have often occurred as a result of leaking ships' side valves and manifold connections, tank overflows, and hose fractures caused by excessive pressurisation or the closure of valves against the liquid flow

* A regular watch system for checking rates and ullages during loading/ discharging and bunkering operations should be laid down. This demarcation

should include shore staff as well as the ship's officers and crew

- A system of record keeping of all cargo, bunkering and tank cleaning operations

- An agreed rate of loading, whether loading cargo or bunkers. Close communications should be established between the vessel and the shore facilities or bunkering barge through which the shore or barge should be kept closely informed of any fluctuations

- There should be an established procedure for the careful transfer of oil/chemicals and bunkers on board during the voyage. In fact, this type of transfer should be treated in the same regard as loading/discharging or bunkering operation

- Careful transfer of bunkers and/or ballast (if applicable) whilst in port in order to counteract any list caused by cargo

- The retention of records of oil/chemicals presently on board the vessel. These records should be kept on the bridge together with the fire envelope and should include such details as the product trade name, the wax content, specific gravity, viscosity, distillation characteristics, etc. in order to assist in the containment or dispersal of the pollutant in the event of a spill, and

- Compliance with the local bunkering and loading/discharging procedures.

B. Other pollutants

The risk of pollution may also arise from the uncontrolled, unauthorised and indiscriminate dumping of sewage and garbage. Whilst many of the practices designed to minimise oil pollution as listed in the previous section can also be practically applied to the control of shipboard sewage/garbage, additional steps could include:

- The appointment of a supervising crew member designated to be in charge of the collection, containment, segregation and disposal of garbage. One person (probably an engineer) should be designated to be in charge of the ship's sewage system

- Proper procedures should be established for the removal of garbage from the various shipboard departments to a centralised containment area

- Careful records should be maintained of the quantities and types of sewage/garbage retained on board and accumulated from time to time

- There should be clear instructions as to when, where and how the different types of garbage may be properly disposed. The supervising crew members in charge of sewage and garbage must be fully conversant with the MARPOL regulations

- Careful records should be maintained of the garbage disposed to shore and/or incinerated. Receipts and invoices should be retained where possible.

Whilst the above two sections would appear to cover the principle causes of pollution in the marine environment, neither the shipowner, nor shipboard staff should forget that other possible sources include the emission of exhaust gas from a ship's power plant and the ever increasing awareness of noise pollution. Careful monitoring and control of these forms of pollution combined with a full knowledge of the various regulations will undoubtedly assist in preventing possible pollution incidents.

Procedures in the event of a pollution incident

In the event of an oil pollution incident, however minor, it is important for Masters to follow carefully, the instructions contained in the **SHIPBOARD OIL POLLUTION EMERGENCY PLAN (SOPEP)**. The SOPEP has been drafted to comply with the provisions of MARPOL 73/78 and although this International Convention does not apply worldwide, it is nevertheless an extremely useful guide to follow when the vessel is involved in a pollution incident. Under the provisions of MARPOL 73/78, every oil tanker of 150 gt and above, and every vessel other than an oil tanker of 400 gt and above, must carry an approved SOPEP before the vessel may enter the port of a country that has ratified the MARPOL convention.

Similarly, vessels required to carry a **VESSEL RESPONSE PLAN (VRP)** in order to comply with the provisions of the US Oil Pollution Act, 1990, **must** ensure that the reporting of incidents is in strict accordance with the approved vessel response plan on board. It is advisable, that the relevant section of the plan relating to the particular port of call is clearly marked, prior to port entry, in order that it can be referred to quickly in an emergency.

In addition to following the requirements of the VRP and/or the SOPEP, the Master should consult the local P&I club representative. The representative will advise on the steps which should be taken to inform the local authorities and will make arrangements for legal representation and attendance of surveyors if necessary. The representative will also assist the Master in dealing with the local authorities.

It is imperative that the Master and crew co-operate fully with the authorities and **show concern** regardless of the extent of the pollution. If the authorities request permission to board the vessel, the Master should attempt to obtain the advice of a legal representative, via the local P&I representative, before granting permission. In some cases the authorities may have the right, or be able to obtain a court order, or similar compulsory order, to be given access to the vessel. It is therefore important not to be obstructive. At the same time it is important to ensure that the authorities' actions are within the powers granted to them and this can be ascertained by reference to a local legal representative. If this is not possible, and the authorities insist on boarding the vessel, the Master should allow them supervised access to the vessel. However, if access to the vessel is provided to the authorities, the Master should make a note of the time and date, their names, the government department which they represent, and a note of their activities while on board. If the authorities wish to conduct interviews or take statements from the Master or crew, it is important that such interviews are conducted in the presence of a local P&I Club or legal representative. In any event, the Master should ascertain whether the Master and crew have the right to be legally represented before such interviews or statements are taken.

The Master should also ensure that steps are taken to prevent further pollution, and if possible to contain, clean-up and/or remove the pollutant from the area of pollution. Therefore, immediate action is essential. Steps to prevent further pollution may include cleaning up the pollutant on deck and transfer of pollutant into available tanks or spaces. The P&I Club representative will be able to assist the Master on deciding what action is suitable and necessary.

It is of significant assistance to shore personnel involved in the clean-up operation following a liquid cargo spill or bunker spill, that the Master obtain calculations of the relative quantities of the potential pollutant on board, in the pipeline and in the shore tank or bunker barge (as applicable). These quantities will also be of importance in avoiding a costly overestimation of the spill.

Finally, the use of certain dispersants/neutralising agents may be prohibited in certain parts of the world, it is critical therefore that the Master should ensure that before any dispersants/neutralising agents are used, local authorisation is obtained.

Evidence required from the vessel

In order to defend claims of pollution and to prevent further incidents, owners and their insurers will require a detailed account of how the incident occurred, steps taken to prevent the incident and the efforts made to minimise damage. Such an account should be supported by the items of evidence below, and the Master should ensure that such information and documents are retained and available. This information includes the following:

- Log books, cargo work books, rough note books etc. in which the following information should be recorded:

  - Date, time and place where the pollution incident occurred
  - The weather conditions and the state of the tide at the time of the pollution incident
  - Operations being carried out at the time of the spill and the grades/types of pollutant involved. If the pollution incident is caused by broken equipment on board the vessel, the broken parts should be preserved
  - The quantity of pollutant which went overboard and the quantity spilled on deck
  - The extent of pollution, the area covered by the spill and whether it has or may effect other property or vessels
  - Details of the actions taken on board the vessel and on shore to contain and clean-up the pollutant
  - The equipment used to contain and clean-up the pollutant including the type, industrial name and quantity of the oil dispersant or any other chemical used. An inventory of the cleaning materials, dispersants and absorbent material on board the vessel should always be kept
  - Actions taken to report the pollution incident, not only to the vessel owners, but

also to the statutory authority. Careful records should also be kept in the vessels radio log of all W1, RT, VHF and Satcom exchanges, and
- The identity of any vessels in the vicinity when the pollution incident occurred.

- Samples of the pollutant which has been spilled

- Video film and/or still photographs of the extent of the spill (if possible)

- Accounts of the events from all the members of crew involved in the incident

- The official log book in which the Master should have recorded all the relevant facts, not opinions or conjecture

- All relevant telexes, cables and other communications/correspondence

- The cargo loading/discharging plan

- Tank and pipe line diagrams including sounding pipe and ullage plug diagrams

- Owner's/charterers' instructions

- Refinery or shore installation instructions or, where applicable, a copy of the bunker supplier's instructions or delivery note containing an agreed loading rate

- The Vessel Response Plan (VRP) and Ship Board Oil Pollution Emergency Plan (SOPEP)

- The vessel's OIL RECORD BOOK, which should always be kept up-to-date.

As a matter of routine, regardless of whether or not there has been a pollution incident, the deck log book should always record:

- The use of such equipment as scupper plugs and drip trays

- The procedures that are followed during the transfer of potential pollutants within the vessel

- The carrying out of oil spill drills and other related exercises, and

- Evidence of any pollution incident, which has been witnessed by the shipboard staff (whether or not own vessel is involved).

Engine room log books should, as a matter of routine, record the following:

- Bunkering procedures

- The members of the crew in charge of bunkering operations

- Methods of effecting emergency stops for bunkering operations

- The times and results of inspections of equipment used in cargo and bunkering operations, and

- A record of the ullages taken during bunkering operations.

Whilst a large percentage of the above list is geared towards oil/chemical

71

pollution incidents, many of the points raised are also applicable to any other form of pollution. It should be noted that in light of the increased public awareness of the potential risk of pollution and damage to the environment a strict regime of control and supervision with authorised safe disposal of other potential pollutants such as garbage and sewage should be installed and strictly maintained.

Careful checks on the proper working efficiency of shipboard systems can also reduce and remove the risk of pollution to the environment through exhaust gas emission and noise generation.

INTERNATIONAL REGULATIONS

A. MARPOL 73/78

All vessels except oil tankers of less than 150 gt and non-tank vessels of less than 400 gt must comply with the International Convention for the Prevention of Pollution from Ships (the "Convention") and the Protocol known as MARPOL 73/78 made pursuant to the convention, when trading in countries which are parties to the Convention. In outline, the Convention lays down requirements relating to:

- The discharge of oil or oily water mixture in parts per million of oil with reference to the distance travelled during discharge

- Segregated ballast systems in oil tankers - IGS and COW

- Adequate reception facilities in ports for oil residues from ships

- The keeping of proper records with regard to oil transfers and tank cleaning

- Mandatory reporting requirements.

B. OPA 90

All vessels which handle, store or transport oil in bulk as cargo, or cargo residue, operating in the navigable waters of the United States **must** carry a response plan which meet the requirements of the VRP regulations and has been approved by the United States Coast Guard. It is important that Masters are familiar with the VRP, particularly the reporting procedures as a failure to comply with the reporting procedures **will** have serious consequences upon the shipowner's right to rely upon defences under OPA 90.

CASE STUDY - 1

A VLCC scheduled for drydocking was carrying out a transfer of slops and a final wash of the last slop tank, immediately prior to docking. This was taking place Off Port Limits near Singapore.

The VLCC took all usual precautions prior to a transfer of oil, as per ISGOTT recommendations. In addition, the carrying capacity of the slop barge was obtained, in writing, and a suitable entry made in the log book.

During the transfer, the slop barge overflowed one of its tanks, and because there were no scupper plugs in (the slop barge), there was an escape of oily water to the sea. A passing patrol vessel observed the pollution, and both vessels were initially charged with causing a pollution.

However, photographs were taken from the VLCC, which clearly showed the slop barge's tank overflowing, and the fact that none of its scupper plugs were in. On the basis of this conclusive evidence, the VLCC was absolved of all blame and the charges dropped.

CASE STUDY - 2

A ULCC built in 1977 and without fully segregated ballast, was loading in an Arabian Gulf port. As required by local regulations, the vessel was loading and discharging simultaneously. The ballast consisted of clean sea water loaded into cargo tanks, which was segregated from the incoming oil by at least two valve separation. However, cargo lines containing oil passed through the tanks containing water.

Despite MARPOL recommendations, no ballast reception facilities exist at this port, and all ballast is discharged to the sea.

When the ballast tanks were getting close to empty, a sheen of oil was seen on the surface of the sea. This rapidly worsened, and deballasting was stopped. The vessel ultimately had to sail with over 5,000 m^3 of water on board, and was fined \$25,000 plus clean-up costs.

At the time of the pollution incident, it was impossible to ascertain the cause of the pollution. Six weeks later, after discharging in the US Gulf, it was possible to enter the tanks for an inspection.

It was found that a hole had developed in one of the lines loading oil, allowing oil to contaminate the ballast. This line had been pressure tested during the previous ballast voyage, and found to be tight. Unfortunately due to the age of the vessel this kind of material failure is always going to be a risk.

This type of incident is quite prevalent, and can take place even on the most modern of tankers. It is one in which evidence in mitigation is very difficult to obtain at the time of the incident, and invariably is blamed on the ship's staff. Evidence of mechanical or material failure obtained after the event, (in many cases weeks later), is usually too late, as all blame, fines, etc. are usually already apportioned.

Chapter Eight

GENERAL AVERAGE

Introduction

The principles of general average have evolved from ancient times as a means of compensating parties with a common interest in maritime venture, if property has to be sacrificed or expenditure incurred, to save the venture as a whole. From its simple origin as an agreement between merchants, general average has matured into a complex branch of shipping law governed by precise rules and conventions.

This chapter deals with the following:

What is General Average?

Who are interested parties and how is General Average assessed?

When is General Average declared?

Ship agents and surveyors

The Master's role.

What is general average?

The main principles of general average are contained in the York-Antwerp Rules, 1994. The Rules define a general average act as follows:

> *"There is a general average act when, and only when, any extraordinary sacrifice or expenditure is intentionally and reasonably made or incurred for the common safety for the purpose of preserving from peril the property involved in a common maritime adventure."*

In the context of marine insurance, the word "average" means a partial loss. General average must be distinguished from "particular average" which means an insured loss. For example, if fire is discovered on board a laden vessel, the following items make up the general average loss:

- Cost of damage caused by water or any other methods used to extinguish the fire

- Cost of repair if ship's structure has to be altered to gain access to fire

- Value of any cargo damaged or jettisoned during efforts to control fire

- Cost of using the ship's equipment and the wages of the crew during the general average incident.

In another example, if a vessel runs aground in a dangerous position, the following items would make up the general average loss:

- Cost of tugs to refloat the vessel, including the value of any salvage award

- Cost of running ship's engines and other equipment to assist refloating

- Cost of discharging cargo into lighters and the cost of reloading

- Cost of pollution removal if cargo has been jettisoned and the value of the lost cargo

- Stores consumed and wages paid to crew during the general average incident.

It is important to note that items of particular average are not calculated as part of the general average loss. In the grounding situation, for example, damage caused to vessel as a consequence of the grounding would not be a part of the general average loss, but would form a hull and machinery claim.

Who are the interested parties and how is general average assessed?

The general average incident will necessarily involve some part of the cargo or ship being sacrificed or extra expenditure being incurred to save the entire venture. The interested parties to the maritime venture, normally the shipowner, the cargo owner, and the charterer, will compensate the party who has suffered the general average loss by making contributions in proportion to the value of their relative interests in the venture as a whole.

The **shipowner's** interest in the venture is determined by the current value of the vessel at the termination of the venture. Time charter hire is normally excluded from owner's total interest but may be included depending on the terms of the charter. In voyage charters, the amount of bunkers onboard would be included in the shipowners valuation.

The **time charterer's** interest in the venture is determined by the value of bunkers remaining onboard at the time of the incident, plus the freight at risk on the voyage.

The **cargo owner's** interest is determined by the sound market value of the cargo on the last day of discharge.

The assessment of each party's contribution is called an "average adjustment". In recent times, the principles by which an adjustment is made are generally governed by the "York-Antwerp" Rules, 1994. The rules ensure that all average adjustments conform to an international standard.

The adjustment is made by an **average adjuster**. The average adjuster is appointed by the shipowner to collect all the facts surrounding the incident and to collect guarantees from various parties before cargo is discharged. The adjuster will have all the facts and figures at his disposal, and thus, in addition to calculating the contributions due from each party, he will be frequently requested to adjust any resulting hull claim.

When is general average declared?

The declaration is normally made by the shipowner, but in certain countries any one of the interested parties may initiate an adjustment. A declaration must be made before the delivery of the cargo. Shipowners usually will allow delivery of the cargo when the other interested parties to the venture provide suitable security sufficient to cover their contribution.

Ship agents and surveyors

Following a general average incident, ship agents and surveyors play a significant role. A ship agent, in addition to the normal duties of port and husbandry agency, will assist the Master in the aftermath of a general average incident to make a declaration which complies with the local law and custom of the port. Once the average adjuster has confirmed that security has been obtained from all the interested parties, the agent is instructed by the shipowner to permit delivery of the cargo. If cargo has been discharged to lighten the vessel, or cargo has been transhipped to a final destination, the agent will be responsible for keeping full and complete records of all movements and expenditure attributable to the general average.

After any incident, a large number of surveyors representing various interests will descend on the vessel. Some of these surveyors will not be involved directly in the general average process, for example, those acting on behalf of hull underwriters, the classification society, or state officials. However, if it has become necessary to sacrifice or discharge a part of the cargo before arrival at the final destination stated on the bill of lading, the shipowner will appoint surveyors to report on the condition and quantity of cargo. Such surveyors, usually called general average surveyors, will act in the interests of all the parties involved (and may also represent hull and machinery interests). If possible, the account representing expenditure incurred should be examined and approved by the general average surveyor before settlement.

On the other hand, surveyors appointed by cargo interests only represent the interests of their client. They may criticise the action taken by the Master or allege that the vessel was unseaworthy (unseaworthiness is discussed in detail in Chapter 1). Therefore, if an incident occurs which may give rise to a general average act and, if time permits (for example, in a grounding incident), the Master should consult owners and cargo interests to discuss the best possible course of action. Prior consultation may resolve disagreements and help to avoid later disputes.

The Master's role

The Master must be prepared to assume the widest possible role in solving all the problems created by an incident if there is an urgent need to do so and assistance is not readily available. Apart from good seamanship and reasonable judgement, the Master must ensure that the history of the incident is recorded accurately and fully. The record should include details of all actions taken by the various parties involved and include their names and organisations. If possible, the Master should ensure that a photographic record of the events is made. The Master's evidence will be crucial as it is usual for a year or more to elapse between the incident and issue of the "Statement of General Average".

If salvage services are involved, the Master should ensure that a full record is made of the salvor's actions and the equipment used. This evidence, together with an assessment of the dangers involved, will determine the level of the salvage award (further information on salvage may be found in Chapter 9).

In most cases of general average, the main evidence for the adjustment is obtained from the various survey reports. The Master should ensure that a clear and accurate account of events is given to surveyors. The survey reports will be supported by witness statements and the vessel's records. When draft surveys and other calculations are being performed, it is advisable for the Master to ensure that a responsible officer is on hand to guide and assist the surveyor.

Examples of documentation used to prepare the adjustment are as follows:

- Casualty reports prepared by the Master
- Survey reports prepared by attending surveyors
- Log extracts and other available records from the vessel
- Copies of communications/instructions relating to the incident
- Statements, which are prepared by owner's solicitors, taken from personnel involved in the incident
- Details of all expenses incurred as a consequence of the general average act fully supported by invoices (including onward charges for cargo if transhipped)
- Salvage award
- Copies of all port papers covering the period during which the incident occurred
- Full cargo manifest and valuation information for cargo
- Vessel's valuation adjusted for any damage repairs allowable in general average
- Statement of fuels and stores consumed and labour used during the general average act
- All documentation covering the security provided by all interested parties.

CASE HISTORY

The subject vessel was a large bulk carrier with nine holds and with the bridge, engine room, and accommodation aft. She was let on an NYPE time charter and was carrying a cargo of wheat, loaded in all holds, from the US Gulf to Europe. The general average adjustment in this case was made according to the "York-Antwerp" Rules, 1994.

Day 1

The vessel sailed from the load port during the morning and proceeded downstream under the Master's orders and the pilot's advice. At 1626 hours, the vessel touched bottom. The various attempts to free her using the helm and engines failed. With the assistance of the pilot boat, it was established that the vessel was aground 200 feet to the west of the channel, resting on a bottom of soft mud and silt. It was also established that two channel buoys used to position the vessel were 300 feet west of their charted location. It was calculated that the vessel was 17,000 MT aground.

Owners retained a local Salvage Master and tugs to try and free the vessel.

Days 2-4

Three attempts to free the vessel using up to eight tugs failed. The owners terminated the services of the local Salvage Master.

Days 5-13

During this period, a local firm was contracted to remove a portion of the cargo with vacuvators into a lightering vessel, chartered by owners. Due to the poor performance of the vacuvators and a dispute over the employment of stevedores, this method was abandoned. The small amount of cargo discharged was reloaded. An international salvage company was then retained to take charge of the operation on the basis of cost plus fifteen percent. A program was planned to dredge a channel from the bow of the vessel to the main navigational channel and also to create a channel along the port side of the vessel. Additional dredging was proposed around the ship's side to break the suction imposed by the mud.

Days 14-20

The dredging operations were commenced and completed.

Day 21

Five tugs were engaged to pull the vessel into the dredged channel and into the main channel. The attempt failed as the ground reaction was too great to allow the vessel to float free.

Days 22-27
All the interested parties agreed that the best course of action was to discharge 17,000 MT of cargo to enable the vessel to refloat. A crane barge and two cargo barges were located, inspected, and brought to the vessel.

Days 28-36
The discharge of the cargo into approved barges began. The parties decided to load both barges while the weather was fine rather than risk a twenty-four hour delay in a refloating attempt in which time the weather may have deteriorated.

Day 37
A total of 15,000 MT of cargo was discharged. Four tugs were engaged, and the vessel was successfully refloated.

Days 38-43
The vessel berthed at the nearest facility which could accommodate her for reloading of the discharged cargo. Extensive survey work was undertaken to ensure that no damage had occurred to the hull, machinery, or cargo during the grounding. After bunkering, the vessel sailed for her original destination.

The following parties were involved in this particular salvage operation:

Owners' representatives and Master - from owners' staff

Salvage Association representative - hull and machinery underwriters

Salvage Association representative - loss of hire underwriters

Independent surveyor to represent general average interests

Independent surveyor - cargo underwriters

Salvage Master - owners' consultant

Class surveyor - vessel's classification society

Ship's agent - local co-ordination and representation

Contractors' representatives - various firms involved throughout operation

Local state officials - environment interests.

During all stages of the discharge and reloading operation, a strict watch was kept on the condition, quantity, and quality of the cargo. The resulting surveys showed that 90 MT of cargo had been lost during handling, and that 20 MT had been contaminated by water in the barges. The value of the lost cargo was made good in the adjustment and credited to cargo owners. The value of the contaminated cargo was made good by a claim on distressed cargo underwriters.

- The expenditure allowed in the general average adjustment included the following:

- Cost of pilotage/towage and launch service

- Salvage Master's fees and expenses

- Cost of helicopter services and local transportation

- Hire of vacuvators/equipment and labour

- Charter expenses for lightering vessel

- Insurance premiums for all stages of the operation (cargo, vacuvators, disbursements, and other vessels)

- Hire of dredging equipment

- Agent's fees and expenses

- Expenses incurred obtaining permits and clearance from the local authorities

- Owners', surveyors' and representatives' fees and expenses

- Salvage company's fees and expenses

- Hire of floating barges and equipment

- Port charges incurred during reloading operation

- Stevedores' fees as per union rules

- Cost of underwater survey and diver services

- Legal fees and expenses incurred during negotiations with stevedores

- Wages and provisions of Master, officers and crew

- Cost of fuel, diesel oil, water, and stores used by vessel during efforts to refloat

- Allowance for cargo lost during handling

- Cost of valuation of the vessel

- Payment to owners for assistance in assembling documents and accounts

- Cost of adjustment, printing, and miscellaneous expenses, and

- Cost of salvors' mark up on direct expense (15%).

Total amount of extraordinary expenditure

The total amount of extraordinary expenditure incurred as a consequence of the general average act was $3,175,143.44. The adjustment was as follows:

Contributing Interests and Appointment of General Average

		Contributory Value	General Average
Vessel:	Value in sound condition	$14,600,000.00	$1,430,938.26
Freight:	None at risk		
Cargo:	Delivered value of 75,978.39 MT of wheat	$17,775,236.77	
	Amount made good - 90 MT	$21,055.50	
		$17,796,292.27	$1,744,205.18
		$32,396,292.27	$3,175,143.44

Chapter Nine

SALVAGE

Introduction

"Salvage" is payment made or due to a salvor for saving of a ship and/or its cargo from loss, damage, wreck, capture, or rescue of property from fire.

A salvor is any vessel or person who renders salvage services to a vessel, and may include pilots, foyboatmen and others who provide equipment to render the services. The salvor must volunteer consequently when specifically engaged, naval personnel, port authorities, or the crew of the salved vessel may all be excluded from claiming salvage as they may be under a public or private duty to assist the vessel.

There are three basic criteria which must be met for services to be regarded as salvage:

Firstly, the object of the salvage should be in danger, although not necessarily imminent danger.

Secondly, the services rendered by salvors must be beneficial to the salved property.

Thirdly, the services must be successful (although there is an exception to this in respect of claims under Article 14 of the Salvage Convention which relate to circumstances where there is a threat of damage to the environment).

This chapter examines the following:

The Salvage Contract

The evidence required from the Master in different circumstances where salvage services are rendered

Main engine breakdown

Grounding

Collision

Fire

War Damage.

The salvage contract

Salvage services do not need to be rendered under contract provided that they meet the three criteria above. Most salvage services are conducted on Lloyd's Open Form (LOF) which is a no cure no pay agreement.

LOF is designed to expedite the saving of property in danger as there is no possibility of debate about the amounts payable to salvors at the time of danger. If subsequently the parties cannot agree to the reward due under the LOF, the matter is placed before an arbitrator chosen by the Committee of Lloyds.

The arbitrator after consideration of all the available evidence makes a salvage award which he believes fair and just to all parties concerned. In cases of salvage not governed by contract, the amount of the award will usually be decided by a court.

Payment of the salvage award is made to the salvors. The parties with an interest in the property salved make contributions to the award in proportion to the salvaged value of their interest.

If salvage services are required and if time allows, it is important that the Master informs his owners as soon as a casualty occurs to prevent the salvage services becoming more urgent and consequently more expensive.

The London Salvage Convention 1989 gives the Master authority to conclude a salvage contract on behalf of the owners of the vessel and on behalf of those who have property on board, namely the cargo owners and possibly charterers.

However, the convention does not apply in some countries and the Master may not have this authority. Therefore, where time and circumstances permit, the owners or the Master should obtain the authority of the cargo owners and charterers before agreeing to the terms on which the salvage services will be rendered. Where it proves impossible to contact them or where there is insufficient time because of the circumstances or urgency of the situation, the Master himself may negotiate the terms of the salvage agreement with the salvors, subject to the owner's standing instructions. From a practical point of view the Master will not normally know, in the heat of the moment, whether the convention applies to his circumstances or not. The safest course of action, therefore, is to assume that it does not apply and to try to seek cargo owners and charterer's agreement before agreement to salvage services unless the matter is urgent and the time taken to obtain that agreement would greatly increase the risk to the ship and cargo.

Finally, it is important to note that most salvage agreements, including the LOF, require full co-operation between the crew of the salved vessel and the salvors. Although there may be substantial tension between the two parties, the Master should ensure that his crew fully assist and co-operate with the salvors.

Evidence required from the vessel

It is important to note that the type of evidence listed in this section will be relevant whether the Master finds his vessel in a position to render salvage services or whether the vessel is the recipient of such services. The evidence required from the vessel will depend on the circumstances in which salvage services are rendered and particular situations are discussed below.

However, there are certain crucial items of evidence which will be required in all claims involving salvage, and therefore, if a casualty occurs, the Master should follow the procedures listed on next page:

Procedures

- Ensure that an accurate record is kept of any conversations relating to a salvage agreement. If at all possible, where an agreement is reached by radio, an independent third party should be asked to take notes for future reference

- Ensure that a precise record is kept of the time of the commencement of salvage services, the times of any communication relating to salvage agreements, and time of arrival of salvage vessels

- Delegate a record keeper or clerk whose task it is to fully and accurately record events in writing, by photographs, or any available method; including any discussion with salvors as to methods proposed

- Ensure that deck, engine and radio log books are accurate and current, and in particular the deck logs contain regular records of the vessel's position.

Masters often prepare a factual account of an incident shortly afterwards. This is usually in the form of a report to the owners or an aide memoire to assist in the preparing of the statements. This is clearly a useful practice but such a factual account should be in addition to detailed records set out above and not in place of them.

In addition to the above items, in the following situations where salvage services may be required, the record keeper should keep a note of the items listed below. (Some of them may be relevant to other sections and the list below should not be seen as comprehensive).

Main Engine Breakdown

- The vessel's position, recorded at frequent intervals

- The extent of damage and the prospects of repairing the engine unassisted, and the crew's ability to complete such repairs

- The prospects of repair at sea or in a port of refuge

- The windforce and direction and tidal or other currents together with all weather forecasts

- If the vessel has to be towed, details of the tow, the distance towed, any difficulties on the tow, and the weather conditions during the tow including video film or photographs, and

- The identity of any alternative salvors.

Grounding

- The nature of the bottom, the manner in which the vessel went aground, and soundings taken around the vessel at regular intervals

- The vessel's position and her heading when she grounded

- The prospects of refloating the vessel unassisted

- Whether or not the vessel is being driven further aground

- Whether or not the vessel's auxiliaries and main engine are available for use

- Details of the pre-stranding draft of the vessel and the draft when she went aground with particular reference to tidal conditions

- Any indication that the vessel is moving whilst aground

- Whether or not the vessel is hogging or sagging

- Details of any cargo damage

- The extent of damage to the vessel, if any

- Details of any personal injuries

- Weather conditions including the wind direction

- Weights on board the vessel and where carried, together with copies of all calculations of the ship stability

- Condition and contents of tanks at regular intervals

- Details of any pollution

- Details of other tugs or other vessels assisting to refloat the vessel and the length of time they were engaged in pulling the vessel, and

- Details of lightering operations, including the number of gangs used, the names of lightering vessels, the vessel's draft on commencement and completion of lightering, and the amount of cargo discharged. Details and causes of cargo lost/damaged during transshipment

- In addition the Master should retain a copy of divers' reports on the condition of the vessel's bottom.

Collision

- The condition of the vessel and the extent of damage

- If there was an ingress of sea water, the areas of the vessel which were flooded, the attempts made to seal openings, whether or not the doors were water tight

- Details of any personal injuries

- Calculation of the ship stability

- Details of any cargo damage

- Whether or not the vessel's pumps, generators and auxiliary machinery remain operable

- Whether or not there is a danger of the vessel sinking, and

- The equipment used by salvors
- In addition, the Master should retain a copy of any reports made by surveyors or naval architects
- Details of any pollution.

Fire

- Where on the vessel the fire started and the extent of damage
- What combustible material is there on board the vessel which the fire may reach
- Details of any cargo damage
- Attempts made by the crew to extinguish the fire including details of the use of foam, CO_2, or portable pumps (including calculation of the ship's stability which is carried out to determine which fire fighting options are available)
- Details of any personal injuries
- If available, readings of explosimeters, and
- Whether or not there is a danger of explosion and whether or not the tanks are gas free or inerted
- If tugs and other fire fighting craft involved, their names, positions, and details of their fire fighting operations
- The position of monitors and hoses, and
- The time taken to extinguish the fire.

If the fire is serious, a fire expert will probably be appointed by owners as soon as possible to determine the cause of the fire and possibly advise on fire fighting methods. The Master should ensure that the area where the fire started is disturbed as little as possible.

War

- Details of the current war situation in the area
- Whether or not the attack on the vessel is part of a campaign
- Details of the last attack on a merchant vessel, and
- The chances of a second strike
- Details of any personal injuries
- Details of any cargo damage
- The Master should ensure that the Salvage Association is informed of any attacks and the extent of the damage
- Details of any pollution.

LOF 90, LOF 95 and the 1989 Salvage Convention, also contain provisions for the payment of an award of special compensation to salvors in circumstances where there was a threat of damage to the environment. This can occur where the amount which would normally be awarded as salvage is less than the salvors' expenses of the whole salvage operation plus a reasonable margin. This is usually because the ship and cargo have little or no value at the time of completion of the operation. Awards for special compensation are paid only by the shipowner (or his P&I club) and not by owners of other property on board.

In cases where there is a risk of damage to the environment, however remote, a comprehensive record of all salvors' activities (not just those related to pollution) should be kept. This record should include full details of all equipment and men used on a daily basis, and will enable shipowners' solicitors to check salvors' evidence of their expenses.

Chapter Ten

COLLISIONS

Introduction

This chapter examines the type of evidence required where the ship has been involved in a collision. It is likely that in the aftermath of a collision, lawyers and surveyors acting for owners and their insurers will come aboard the vessel and play an active role in gathering evidence necessary to bring or defend claims for damage. However, they will rely heavily on the Master and the crew to provide much of the evidence.

This chapter deals with the following:

Evidence required prior to a collision -
   Working charts
   Movement books
   Log book - regular entries

Evidence required after a collision -
   General
   Vessel under pilotage or in congested waters
   Vessel moored or anchored

Involvement of lawyers

A case study will be found in Appendix 10:1. The reader should also refer to chapters 8 and 9 in the event that salvage services are required or a general average incident occurs as a result of the collision.

Evidence prior to a collision

Evidence recording the daily routine of the vessel will be crucial in determining how and why a collision occurred. This type of evidence will include copies of the vessel's rough log books. It is imperative, therefore, that all sections of the log book are completed fully and accurately at all times (refer to the introduction of this book). Sounding records are also likely to be important.

Working charts and movement books are two items of evidence which have particular relevance in collision investigations.

Working charts

The Master should ensure that chart positions are left precisely as plotted and that positions which do not match others are not erased. As a large number of collisions occur under pilotage or in congested waters, the Master should also ensure that the general practice of marking the ship's position on charts during the passage is continued while the vessel is under pilotage. Particular care should be taken to plot the vessel's location on the chart, for example, by indicating the distances abeam off buoys.

Movement books

The Master should ensure that movement books are kept in ink and that any alterations are made in ink, signed, and dated by the person making the alterations. The material deleted should be scored out with a single line leaving the writing underneath legible. The use of correction fluid should not be permitted.

The Master should also ensure that times are recorded as accurately as possible. Finally, he should ensure that printer outputs from telegraph recorders and the engine room are retained as part of the movement book.

Evidence after a collision
General

If possible, the Master and the crew should collect, record, and preserve as much detail of the collision as they can immediately after an incident. Although a comprehensive list of the items of evidence required from the vessel is provided at the end of this chapter, the type of evidence discussed below is of particular importance. The Master should ensure that a note of the following is made:

- The vessel's position at the time of the incident -

  Every effort should be made to fix and confirm the position from more than one source

- The exact time of the collision -

  The accuracy of the clocks on the bridge and in the engine room as well as the accuracy of automatic recorders such as course recorders, telegraph loggers, and data loggers should be verified. The personal watches of the members of the crew who witnessed the incident should be checked. If a reflective plotter was in use prior to a collision, the crew member operating the plotter should ensure that he has made a note (not on the screen) of any marks he made on the screen with the time they were made

- The heading of the vessel at the time of the collision -

  It is important that the course recorder is marked in ink to indicate the time when the vessel collided, although care should be taken not to spoil the trace. If a course recorder is not available, the heading of the vessel should be determined by some other method which also should be recorded

- An estimate of the angle of blow by or to the other vessel

- An estimate the speed of each of the vessels at the time of the collision -

  The estimates can be verified at a later date by other data such as photographs and logs

- Any alterations of course and speed prior to a collision -

If possible, this note should be verified by a second person or equipment recording.

In addition, the Master should ensure that all crew members on the bridge as well as other members of the crew who witnessed the incident, record their account of events which occurred prior to and after the incident. The Master should also ensure that any independent witnesses to the incident are identified. He should record the names of all the vessels in the vicinity and attempt to obtain the names and addresses of the operators and duty officers of these vessels by VHF.

Finally, the Master should ensure that any scraps of paper which have been disposed of in the waste paper basket on the bridge are retained as these may contain the key as to why and how a collision occurred.

Vessel under pilotage or in congested waters

As stated above, many collisions take place when a vessel is under pilotage or in congested waters. In such cases, the actions of the person controlling the vessel immediately before the vessel was involved in a collision, are particularly relevant in determining the cause of the collision. The Master, in addition to gathering the evidence discussed in the preceding sections, should ensure that the watch keeper, helmsman, the look-out, and any other persons on the bridge at the time of the collision make a complete record of events. The pilot also should be requested to make a written account of the events before he leaves the vessel. A note should be made of the pilot's name, address and telephone number.

The Master should record speed log readings and make a note of the state of the tide at the time of the collision. An estimate of tidal current is unlikely to be accurate. However, a note of the time of observed slack water will be useful when calculations are being made from tide tables. The Master should note that S.A.L. logs may be inaccurate in freshwater.

Vessel moored

It is generally the view that unless there is evidence that the moored or anchored vessel contributed in some way to the collision, the vessel underway is liable for the damage.

Regardless of whether the Master is on the colliding vessel, he should ensure the following information is obtained:

- Whether or not the vessel or an adjacent vessel was testing her main engines in such a way as to contribute to the incident

- Whether or not the moorings on the moored vessel were defective, slack or ineffective in any way

- An estimate of the tidal direction and strength

- The identity of witnesses on shore, and

- Photographs of damage to own vessel, and if possible, of the damage to the other vessel.

As many of the incidents which take place when the vessel is moored are minor incidents, the insurers of both vessels may not require a joint survey, but will rely heavily on the Master's evidence. It is important, therefore, that the Master's report of the incident gives a detailed record of the damage.

Involvement of lawyers

As stated above, lawyers are likely to play a significant role in gathering evidence in the aftermath of a collision. While the investigating lawyers are likely to be appointed by the vessel's insurers and will not be directly representing the interests of the Master and crew, these interests do to a certain degree coincide with those of the insurers. Therefore, the lawyers may advise the Master and the crew of their legal position and if the circumstances merit it, recommend that the crew or their union appoint their own lawyers.

Finally, there is an understanding between lawyers that if they represent owners of another vessel, they will not question crew members of the opponent's vessel. Therefore, the Master should ensure that crew members identify any persons to whom they make statements. When a joint survey is arranged, the surveyor appointed on behalf of the other vessel is attending to inspect the physical damage to your vessel. He is not usually authorised to inspect the navigational equipment, log books or interview the crew.

Checklist

- True courses steered during four hours before collision (time, position, altered course to)

  Weather conditions at time of collision:
  - Direction and force of wind
  - Direction and height of sea
  - Direction and height of swell
  - Visibility
  - Last weather forecast

- State of tide and currents

- Personnel on bridge at or immediately before collision and their duties

- Last fix before sighting the other vessel

- Radars in use and what range scales they were set on

- Position fixing system(s) in use and intervals between fixes

- First observation of other vessel:
  - By what means
  - Time

- Distance and bearing
- Lights and shapes observed
- Aspect
- Apparent course

- True course of own ship at time of first observation

- Position of own ship at time of first observation (state how obtained)

- Speed of own ship at time of first observation

- Action taken by own vessel at time of first observation

- Subsequent observations:
  - Times
  - Distance and bearing

- First visual sighting of other vessel
  - Time
  - Distance and bearing
  - Lights observed and shapes
  - Aspect
  - Apparent course
  - Bearing and distance of other vessel when echo was first observed by radar
  - What other lights and shapes (if any) were subsequently seen before the collision

- Steps taken to plot other vessel (eg reflection plot, formal plot)

- Record of actions of both vessels including times up to the time of collision (including engine movement)

- Sound signals made and when made

- Sound signals heard and when heard

- Details of any communications between vessels before collision (eg aldis, VHF)

- Time of collision

- Position of collision (state how obtained)

- Angle of contact between vessels (if possible take photographs or make a drawing)

- Which parts of each vessel first came into contact

- Heading of own vessel at time of collision

- Speed of own vessel at time of collision

- Heading of other vessel at time of collision

- Speed of other vessel at time of collision

- Draught (draft) of own vessel at time of collision

- Description of movements of both vessels after collision

- Details of communications after collision

- Names of other vessels in vicinity when collision occurred

- Communications with other vessels in vicinity

- If vessel under pilotage, name, address and telephone number of pilot - see also the evidence listed in the section 'Vessel under Pilotage or in Congested Waters'

- If the vessel is moored at the time of collision, see the evidence listed in the section 'Vessel Moored'.

In addition to the above information, the Master should ensure that:
- All witnesses of the incident write an account of the collision and the events leading up to the collision

- The practice of marking charts is continued while vessel is under pilotage and chart positions are left precisely as plotted

- Recording telegraph printer output and other printer output from the engine room are retained as part of the movement book

- Accuracy of clocks on bridge and in engine room, as well as automatic recorders are verified

- Course recorder marked in ink to indicate collision

- Operator of reflective plotter makes note of marks

- A full photographic record of events is made

- Scraps of paper on which course calculations may have been made are retained.

- Finally, the Master should ensure that the following general information is noted:
- Details of vessel
  - Name
  - Nationality
  - Port of registry
  - Vessel's general description
  - Radio equipment on board
  - Vessel's complement (details of rank and qualifications)
  - Watchkeeping arrangements
  - Navigational equipment on board

- Name and port of registry of other ship

- Date of collision

- Cargo on board at time of collision (ie nature and tonnage)

- Approximate area of collision

- Time Zone

- Details of voyage of own vessel:
  - From where to where was the vessel going
  - Time of sailing
  - Draughts (drafts) on sailing (forward, mid and aft)
  - Intended course to next port.

Appendix 10:1

CASE HISTORY

"A", the vessel involved in this incident, was a small sludge carrier. She collided with "B", another vessel, in thick fog in the vicinity of a large United Kingdom pilot station (the reader should refer to the attached plots which were produced from evidence provided by the vessels involved in the incident).

At 0920 hours, "A" adjusted her course to 273 degrees true on an outward leg of a run to dump sludge. Between 0930 hours and 0935 hours, an echo was observed on radar 10 degrees on starboard bow distance 2.7 miles just west of BR Lanby Buoy. "A" and the echo both appeared to be heading for LF1 light float at the entrance of the main channel. The echo's bearing appeared constant during the next few minutes, and the Master made a number of small alterations of course to starboard amounting in total to 40 degrees. "B" was first sighted 2.3 points on port bow at which time "A" was heading about 313 degrees true. "B" appeared to be heading at right angles to "A" at a distance of about 3 cables. "A" collided with "B" at about 0945 hours in a position estimated to be 8 cables ESE of BR Lanby.

At 0916 hours "B" was following a course of 112 BR Lanby 097 degrees true distance 4.5 miles reduced to half speed. At 0925, her course was altered to 095 degrees true to counteract set. At about 0940, an echo was observed 5 degrees on port bow distance 3 miles. A few minutes later, after speaking to the pilot on the VHF, the Master ordered her course to be adjusted to 102 degrees true to bring LF1 light float right ahead with speed reduced to slow check. The radar echo distance of 2 miles was brought right ahead.

A crew member reported that the echo first moved from right ahead to 40 degrees on starboard bow closing to a distance of 4 cables. Soon after, "A" was seen 50 degrees on starboard bow distance 3 cables. The wheel of "B" was put hard a starboard, and the engines stopped and put full astern.

The collision occurred at 0943 hours according to a clock on "B" as recorded by the chief officer. The Master of "B" recorded the collision as taking place at 0944/0945 hours. The Master also estimated that at this time the BR buoy was at 50 degrees true distance 7 cables.

Although there were independent observers in the vicinity who were engaged in damage control exercises, the data provided by them did not appear to relate to this incident but to two other vessels passing close to one another. The evidence from "A" and "B" did not correlate, and the investigators of the collision had difficulty in ascertaining the cause of the incident.

The owners and insurers of "A" were placed at a considerable disadvantage as "A" could not produce certain items of crucial evidence, which included a working chart, a plot of "B" as it approached ("B" also had not plotted "A" as it approached), and a movement book. In addition, there were no automatic recording devices such as course recorders or data loggers, onboard the vessel. As a result of the lack of evidence, "A" was found to be primarily at fault in causing the loss, and her owners were responsible for the damage suffered to "B".

Detail of collision area

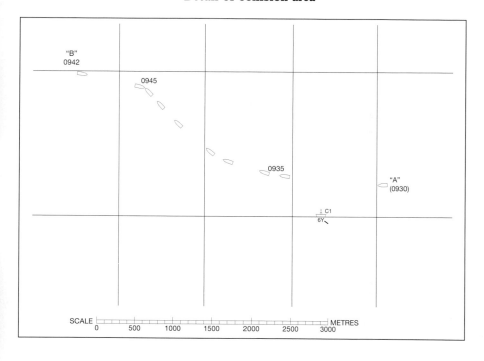

Chapter Eleven

LABOUR DISPUTES AND
DISCIPLINARY PROCEDURES

Introduction

The Master in the course of his duties may be confronted by problems relating to the crew either in the form of collective trade disputes involving strike action or individual disciplinary offences. The legitimacy of such trade disputes and the recourse to disciplinary procedures open to the Master is determined by the law of the flag state. These may be simple civil sanctions or full criminal proceedings. Although the discussion in this chapter of trade disputes on board a vessel and disciplinary procedures is limited to English law (please refer to Appendix 11:1 to this chapter for a discussion as to the position under Greek law and Appendix 11:2 for a discussion as to the position under the law of Cyprus), the principles, especially in relation to the recording of evidence, will be of general application. In addition, this chapter discusses briefly the procedures to be followed by the Master in the event of strike action by shore personnel and also industrial action by the International Transport Workers Federation ("ITF"). Finally, the chapter examines the problems which arise from the growing incidence of drug smuggling on board cargo vessels.

For ease of reference an outline of this chapter is as follows:

Trade disputes -

On board the vessel
ITF disputes
Strikes by shore personnel

Disciplinary procedures

Drug smuggling

In the appendices to this chapter, trade disputes and disciplinary problems are discussed in the context of Greek law and the law of Cyprus.

Trade disputes

Under English law, a trade dispute is a dispute between workers and their own employers which relates wholly or mainly to the conditions of employment, the engagement and non-engagement of workers, allocation of work and duties, discipline, and trade union matters. Industrial action is lawful only if the trade union has obtained the support of its members through a secret and properly conducted ballot.

On board the vessel

A seaman on a United Kingdom registered vessel may leave the ship in contemplation of furtherance of a trade dispute if he has given the Master at least 48 hours' notice. This notice will be valid only if given when the vessel is within the United Kingdom and is securely moored to a safe berth. If the notice is valid, the seaman cannot be compelled to go to sea in the 48 hour period following the giving of the notice even if there are clauses in the crew agreement which prevent him from participating in trade disputes.

Any industrial action on board a United Kingdom ship when the ship is not safely moored in the United Kingdom is a criminal offence. The owners in such a situation may consider bringing criminal charges against the seamen participating in the action.

Whenever there is the likelihood of a trade dispute on board the vessel, the Master should follow carefully all the procedures listed below. The Master should ensure that:

- The seamen's accounts of wages are up-to-date and any payments which are due are made promptly

- All necessary steps are taken to guarantee the safety of all persons on board the vessel and the medical staff are alerted

- As soon as any industrial action is contemplated owners and their local agents are informed and kept closely advised of all developments

- The ship and her equipment are kept in a seaworthy condition in order to allow the vessel to continue the voyage as soon after the resolution of the dispute as possible and all steps taken to maintain the vessel are fully and accurately recorded -

All work on board the vessel should be done in a discrete manner so as not to provoke any incidents with the seamen involved in the industrial action

- The names of the seamen involved in any action are recorded in the official log book -

The record in the log book should set out the full factual details and record what is said, by whom and when. The Master may also consider keeping his own separate record of the factual details surrounding the industrial action in his notebook. This record could then be made available to the owners if they wish to bring any claims against the striking seamen (although the owners arc unlikely to pursue such claims). However, the Master should note that if his notebook is used as evidence, the entire notebook must be made available to the opposing side. Therefore, it is important that such notebooks only contain facts and not opinions or other material which could prejudice owners (please refer to the introduction of this book). It should also be remembered that such note books should supplement any log book entries but it should never replace the formal entries in the log

- In the event that picket lines are set up, the picketers are assured that any officers crossing the picket line are only doing so to reach their living quarters and are not attempting to break the strike

- Before taking the vessel to sea, a full and properly trained and qualified crew are on board and all safety requirements are fulfilled.

Finally, in the interests of all the parties involved, the Master should never participate in any strike of seamen or officers, or attempt to break the strike. If the Master becomes implicated in the strike, the danger exists that local police, military, or company agents will over rule his authority and displace the authority of the Master.

ITF disputes

Since 1972, the ITF has been active in organising boycotts and crew strikes against vessels flying "flags of convenience". The aim of the ITF is to enforce minimum ITF conditions on these vessels relating to wages and terms of employment.

An ITF boycott, or "blacking" as it is sometimes called, occurs when shore personnel, which could include stevedores, lock keepers, boatmen and line handlers, tug crews, and pilots, refuse to provide services to a particular vessel earmarked by the ITF. The shore personnel involved in the boycott usually will belong to an ITF affiliated trade union. The ITF action also may be supported by a crew strike on board.

In order to avoid boycotts against a vessel, many charterers now insist on the owners obtaining a "blue certificate" from the ITF which would exempt the vessel from any ITF action. The effect of the "blue certificate" is that crew agreements are governed by the terms of the current ITF Collective Agreement.

If a boycott is directed against a vessel, it is likely that ITF inspectors will attempt to persuade the Master to enter into an ITF agreement. The Master should immediately inform his owners and ask for full instructions or request owners to send a representative to deal with the demands. Subject to his owner's instructions on the point, the Master may prefer not to sign any document until he has received specific instructions from his owners.

At all stages, the Master should ensure that a full and accurate record of the events is made and that owners are kept fully informed. ITF boycotts are legal in only a few countries, but when they do arise the Master can do very little else but sit out the boycott. A boycott carries less force and is pursued with less enthusiasm by both the strikers and the media if the Master and officers act calmly and are not antagonistic.

Strikes by shore personnel

In the event of strike action on shore, loading and discharging operations on the vessel are likely to be delayed. The wording of any charterparty under which the vessel is operating will determine whether the charterers or the owners will bear the responsibility for any losses incurred as a result of the delay.

As there are likely to be claims arising as a result of the strike with regard to the running of laytime, off-hire, or in the case of a perishable cargo, cargo damage, the Master should contact the local P&I correspondent as soon as possible. If the vessel is carrying a perishable cargo, the claims may be potentially very large, and the P&I correspondent will assist the Master to minimise the damage. The Master may contact the P&I correspondent without any fear of escalating the action being taken on shore as the correspondent will not be a party to the dispute.

If a load or discharge port is named in the bill of lading or similar contract there is an absolute obligation on the Master to take his ship to that port although it is strike bound. However, there is the possibility that the charterparty under which the ship is operating allows for the vessel to load or discharge at an alternative port. If the Master is approaching a port which is strike bound, he should contact owners to discuss this possibility.

While a vessel is in a strike bound port, the Master should ensure that the officers and crew do nothing that will aggravate the dispute. He also should ensure that all the facts relating to the strike are fully and accurately recorded in the log book. This record should include the amount of time lost and any additional expenses incurred by the vessel. In addition, the Master should keep a scrapbook of local newspaper reports of the strike.

Disciplinary procedures

Disciplinary procedures on board a United Kingdom vessel are governed by the Merchant Navy Code of Conduct. This code of conduct allows five sanctions of successively greater intensity which must be used for dealing with disciplinary problems. These sanctions are as follows:

- Informal warning -

  This warning is given for first offences of a minor nature. It usually is given by an officer at an appropriate level lower than the Master and is given immediately with no written record being kept of the incident

- Formal warning -

  This warning is given for more serious offences or for repetition of a minor offence. It is given by the head of department and is recorded in the company files

- Master's formal warning -

  This warning is recorded in the official log book and follows on after the two previously mentioned sanctions, or alternatively it is given for a serious disciplinary offence

- Master's written reprimand -

  This is a last chance warning which is recorded in the official log book. A copy of the reprimand is also given to the offender

- Dismissal -

  This sanction may only be used for the most serious of offences.

Discipline on board a United Kingdom ship, in all cases, should be maintained according to this code of conduct (or any similar codes provided by other flag states). In addition, offences should be dealt with as soon as possible after the event. However, in the case of more serious offences which warrant formal treatment, the Master should wait a few hours after the offence has been committed before disciplining the crew member in question. The Master, thus, will have the opportunity to ascertain all the facts surrounding the incident before he interviews the crew member and he can conduct the interview in an orderly manner.

A disciplinary interview must be conducted in accordance with the rules of natural justice. Thus, the charge against the offender must be read out and both the offender and his accuser must be present throughout the interview. If there is more than one offender, the Master should not take sides, but treat them impartially. The offender should be allowed to be represented by a friend, and any statements made by witnesses will be subject to cross examination. The decision will be made once the offender has been given the chance to make his statement. When a decision has been made, the Master should ensure that all the relevant forms are prepared in the presence of the offender and that all concerned are informed of the decision.

The most common offence committed on board is absence without leave from the place of duty, often in conjunction with being drunk. If a crew member does come on duty under the influence of alcohol, he should be sent to his quarters for his own safety and the safety of others. The Master should ensure that all witnesses make a written statement, testifying to the unsuitable condition of the crew member.

The Master himself should deal with all cases of refusal to obey an order and all cases of fighting so he is aware of the underlying problems which led to the incident. He also should personally deal with crew members who go missing from the ship and later rejoin. All cases dealt with by the Master should be recorded in the official log book. If the vessel incurs extra expenses in the form of hiring replacement labour as a result of the crew member's conduct, the Master may make a suitable deduction from his wages. The Master should ensure that a record is kept of all expenses incurred and deductions made.

The Master, in the case of the most serious offences listed in the code of conduct, may dismiss the offender. The code of conduct provides that the Master may summarily dismiss an offender without any prior warnings in certain circumstances. The Master should only resort to summary dismissal in cases of gross misconduct. Most dismissals will be preceded by at least one recorded warning. In the majority of cases, the Master will dismiss a crew member at the end of the voyage.

Whenever a crew member has been dismissed from the vessel, the Master, in order to counter a possible unfair dismissal claim, should keep a full and accurate record of all warnings both formal and informal given to the crew member over as long a period as possible and a detailed account of the reasons why he was dismissed. In addition, a detailed account should be kept of any expenses deducted from the crew member's wages in order to cover repatriation costs. This account as well as the crew member's account of wages should be entered in the log book.

If a crew member has committed a very serious offence, as defined in the appropriate code of conduct, or the criminal code, dismissal alone may not be sufficient. The Master, in this case, instead of imposing his usual sanctions, should instead refer the offending crew member to the Discipline Organisation ashore. He should collect and document as much evidence as possible to accompany his report. The report and enclosures must then be sent to the appropriate shore discipline organisation and a copy sent to the owners. Another copy must be given to the crew member in question, and a fourth copy placed in the ship's files. A shore based tribunal will conduct an inquiry and decide whether to dismiss the crew member from the merchant marine.

If the crew member has committed a criminal offence or an offence under the Merchant Shipping Acts, the Master and owners may decide to refer the case to the authorities. The Master should ensure that all witnesses make written statements, and a complete account of the incident is entered in the log book with the statements annexed to the log. The entire file must be sent to the owners so they may present the case to the authorities.

Drug smuggling - United States' policy

Drug smuggling on merchant ships has been on the increase during the last decade. Although smuggling occurs in most parts of the world, the largest markets are North America and Western Europe. In some countries such as Malaysia, the death penalty may be imposed on offenders. If drugs are found on a merchant vessel, the ship will be subject to heavy fines, and in some cases, confiscation.

In 1986, the United States adopted a zero tolerance policy towards the carriage of illicit drugs on merchant ships which has placed a heavy financial burden on shipowners and their P&I Clubs. Although confiscation of the vessel and fines for criminal offences are outside the traditional cover provided by P&I insurance, the Clubs generally are prepared to cover owners in cases where there has been no complicity by the owners or their employees.

Drug smugglers have found it increasingly easier to smuggle drugs in merchant ships with little cost to themselves, rather than to use the former methods of speed boats and aeroplanes. In 1986, only 1.7% of the marijuana smuggled into the United States came from merchant ships. By 1988, the amount of marijuana smuggled into the United States in merchant ships had increased to 37.9%. The United States customs in one instance seized as much as 12,000 pounds of cocaine with a street value of almost $100,000,000. The problem has affected all carriers and even the largest and most respectable carriers have found themselves the innocent victims of smugglers.

Under United States law, if drugs are found on a merchant ship, owners will be subject to the penalties mentioned. Owners will be held liable even if the drugs are concealed in a sealed container which, under normal circumstances, would not be opened prior to loading, unless they can show that all possible precautions were taken to prevent smuggling.

The United States customs believes that shipping lines must improve their security to ensure that they are not being used as the unwitting agents of drug smugglers and has been pressing shipping lines to impose strict security measures during loading. In recent years, a total of 256 carriers to the United States have signed a Carriers Initiative Agreement with the authorities under which the carriers undertake to co-operate with customs and to take "the utmost care" to prevent their vessels from being used by smugglers. Under the agreement, shipowners have agreed that the ship's officers will regularly search for narcotics, seal specific compartments on the vessel, provide advance copies of manifests, and assist customs and inform them of any suspicious activity.

The Master should ensure that anything done in connection with the agreement is fully and accurately entered in the log book. Masters and ship's officers should also be aware of the International Chamber of Shipping guidelines on the recognition and detection of drugs.

Appendix 11:1

TRADE DISPUTES AND DISCIPLINARY PROCEEDINGS UNDER GREEK LAW

Trade disputes

Strikes on board Greek cargo vessels are rare as they may be so disruptive as to put the safety of the vessel at risk. The legislation also acts as a powerful deterrent. Under Greek law, industrial action may only take place after a special ballot is called. If no ballot is called, the strike will be illegal and may be banned by the courts. Any form of strike action on board a vessel will result in the suspension of a seaman's contract and a cessation of his wages. Furthermore, the Greek Code of Public Maritime Law provides that strikes by crew members may be considered a mutiny if directed against the Master's authority.

In recent years, there have been several instances of ITF activity directed against cargo vessels flying a flag of convenience, but owned by Greek interests. If an ITF boycott does lead to the Master signing an ITF agreement, crew members may not be able to enforce this agreement. The Greek courts have held that the terms of an ITF agreement are not binding if they have been imposed upon the Master by duress.

As a result of this ruling, the Master should ensure that if his vessel becomes the subject of ITF activity, and he is forced into signing an ITF agreement, he fully and accurately records all events surrounding the ITF boycott and discussions with the ITF representatives.

Disciplinary proceedings

Disciplinary procedures on board a Greek vessel are governed by the Greek Code of Public Maritime Law which imposes four kinds of sanction for disciplinary problems:

1 Reprimand
2 Fine up to one-fifth of the statutory wages
3 Temporary disqualification of licence
4 Permanent disqualification of licence

A reprimand or fine may be imposed by either the Master or the port authorities. If a seaman is fined, he may be refused future employment until he has paid the fine. The crew member may appeal against the Master's decision to the port authorities.

If the Master imposes either of these sanctions, he must make an entry in the "Penal Book" and the official log book. These entries will be vital evidence if the crew member is eventually dismissed for his misconduct and brings a claim for unfair dismissal.

Temporary or permanent disqualifications may only be imposed by the Disciplinary Committee of the Mercantile Marine in the first instance and by the Appellate Disciplinary Committee of Mercantile Marine on appeal.

Under the Greek Code of Private Maritime Law, the Master also has the right to terminate a crew member's contract prematurely and without notice if he has committed a disciplinary offence specified by the Code. The Master's decision to dismiss a crew member must be made as quickly as possible. Otherwise, in a claim for unfair dismissal by the crew member, the Courts may find that either the gravity of the alleged offence is undermined by the Master continuing to accept the offender's services, or the connection between the alleged offence and the dismissal is too tenuous.

If the crew member successfully brings a claim for unfair dismissal, the owners must compensate him by paying him fifteen, thirty, or forty days' wages depending on the remoteness of the port where the seaman has been dismissed.

To defend a claim for unfair dismissal, owners will have to produce the official log book setting out the circumstances of the offence committed and "Penal Book" recording any previous sanctions imposed on the crew member. Unsworn statements from the officers and crew are also useful.

Where a Master has dismissed a crew member, he must make an entry in the "Seafarer's Book" stating the cause of the dismissal. He must be careful to use wording that is as general as possible to avoid becoming the subject of defamation or disciplinary proceedings himself. The following form of wording is recommended:

"The seaman is dismissed by reason of disciplinary offence".

The Master, however, should make a more detailed entry in the official log book describing fully the circumstances of the dismissal. All evidence gathered by the Master in connection with a criminal act committed on board the vessel may be used in future disciplinary proceedings.

If a crew member commits a criminal offence, the Master's authority includes magisterial duties. If the offence is committed while the vessel is at sea, the Master is under a duty to conduct inquiries in order to collect material evidence in connection with the offence. The Master will have to appoint an officer to act as a secretary and take sworn statements from crew members or other persons who witnessed the incident. Any inquiry conducted by the Master in connection with a criminal act in which he was involved, will be void.

In the case of desertion by a crew member, the Master is required to draw up an indictment, setting out the circumstances of the crime. Secretarial duties in drawing up the indictment are carried out by the chief officer if the deserter is a member of the deck crew, or the chief engineer if the deserter is a member of the engine crew.

Although standard forms of the indictment may be obtained from the Ministry of Mercantile Marine, a general statement of the incident is sufficient.

The indictment, accompanied by extracts of the log book describing the desertion and the "Seafarer's Book" are submitted to a port authority or Greek Consulate for transmission to the Ministry of Mercantile Marine or submitted directly to the Ministry. The Ministry will then commence criminal and disciplinary proceedings against the accused seaman, who, if found guilty, faces a sentence of up to one year imprisonment, commutable by fine, and a temporary disqualification of his licence ranging from two to five years.

TRADE DISPUTES AND DISCIPLINARY PROCEEDINGS UNDER CYPRIOT LAW

Trade disputes

By virtue of Article 26 of the Constitution every person has the right to enter freely into any contract subject to such conditions limitations or restrictions as are laid down by the general principles of the contract law of Cyprus. By Article 26(2) of the Constitution and Section 12(6) of the Merchant Shipping (Masters and Seamen) Law No. 46/63 (as amended) Collective Agreements are recognised and may be incorporated into a seaman's employment agreement.

By Article 27 of the Constitution the right to strike is recognised except only for members of the armed forces and the police. Thus any new agreement brought about by the strike action of the crew would be a valid enforceable agreement.

Strikes on board Cypriot flag ship vessels, however, are rare, if not unheard of. But, if due to the activity of a third party, for example by the ITF, directed against a Cypriot flag ship the Master is obliged or forced to sign an ITF collective agreement, a Cypriot court might upon a later recourse to it, find that such an "agreement" had been entered into (in the wording of Section 10(1) of the Cypriot Contract Law Cap 149) without "the free consent of the parties" and thus unenforceable. Such a case has, however, yet to come before a Cypriot Court.

Though Cyprus has not enacted the equivalent of the English trade Unions and Labour Relations Act 1974 the reasoning in the case of THE UNIVERSAL SENTINEL 1980 2 Lloyd's Rep 523 would be highly persuasive in enabling the Court in Cyprus to hold that any agreement reached as a result of ITF action could have resulted from duress.

As a matter of prudence the Master should keep a contemporaneous record in the ship's log book and perhaps in his own note book in greater detail of all the facts and circumstances which led up to his signing any such ITF agreement.

Disciplinary proceedings

Provisions as to discipline on board a Cypriot ship are contained in Sections 75 to 89A inclusive (except for sections 77 and 78 which have been repealed) of the Merchant Shipping (Masters and Seamen) Law and cover such matters as misconduct endangering life or the ship, desertion or absence without leave and general offences against discipline. Such matters, furthermore, constitute criminal offences punishable by imprisonment or fine or both.

In addition to the criminal penalties imposed for the general offences against discipline or for desertion or absence without leave the owner or Master may also impose upon the offender any remedy permitted under the contract of employment for its breach, but on condition, however, that the owner or Master is not compensated more than once in respect of the same damage.

In relation to the commission of any of these offences or for any act of misconduct for which a fine can be imposed and which is to be enforced, then:

a) An appropriate entry has to be made in the official log book signed by the Master and also by the Mate or one other of the crew.
b) If the offender is still in the ship he has to be supplied with a copy of that entry and he is entitled to make a suitable reply which also has to be entered in the official log book and so signed as above.

If in any subsequent legal proceedings the above entries are produced, or proved, the Court may act upon them. If however the entries have not been made as above then the court hearing the case may, in its discretion, refused to hear evidence of the offence or act of misconduct.

Any question concerning the forfeiture of, or deductions from, wages under the law may be determined in any proceedings instituted for that purpose even if the offence concerned has not been made the subject of any criminal proceedings.

Every fine, which has been imposed upon a seaman for any act of misconduct has to be deducted by the Master or owner from the wages of the offender as if the offender had been discharged in the Republic of Cyprus. The offence, and entry in the official log book in respect of that offence, have both to be proved to the satisfaction of the Port Officer before whom the offender is discharged and to whom the fine so imposed has to be paid. An offender who has been so fined and had his fine so deducted from his wages cannot be punished further under the Merchant Shipping (Masters and Seamen) Law.

Whenever in any proceedings relating to a seaman's wages it is shown that a seaman has, in the course of the voyage, been convicted of an offence and rightfully punished by imprisonment or otherwise by a competent tribunal, the Court hearing the case, may direct that an amount not exceeding one month's wages may be applied in reimbursing any costs properly incurred by the Master in procuring the conviction.

If a seaman is discharged without fault justifying such discharge before commencement of the voyage or before one month's wages have been earned, then in addition to his wages, the seaman is entitled to compensation of one month's wages, if discharged in Cyprus, or two months' wages, if discharged outside of Cyprus.

If a seaman without reasonable cause is not paid his wages at the appropriate time that seaman is entitled to two days pay up to a maximum of ten days for which his payment is delayed.

There is, however, in Cyprus no code of conduct similar to the UK Merchant Navy Code of Conduct and a Master of a Cypriot flag ship, if he has not already adopted the UK Code could well do so with advantage. However, the grounds for dismissal are usually provided for in some detail in most standard contracts of employment. Additionally, by Section 13(2) of the Merchant Shipping (Master and Seamen) Law it is provided that a Master may terminate an employment agreement if the seaman fails, without reasonable cause, to join the ship on the date of its signature or, on his unjustifiable absence, at any time. A Master may also dismiss a seaman for grave misconduct endangering the safety of the ship or so as to keep good discipline and order on the ship.

Smuggling

By virtue of Section 31 of the Narcotic Drugs and Psychotropic Substances Law No. 29/77 the Court has power to order the forfeiture of "anything shown to the satisfaction of the Court to relate to the offence", but subject the right of the owner of the thing to be forfeited to be heard. This could cover vessels on which the narcotic substances have been conveyed even without the knowledge of the owner or Master. Under the Customs & Excise Law No. 82/67 provision is also made for the forfeiture of vessels constructed for concealing goods, jettisoning cargo, failing to account for missing cargo and having been signalled to bring to, fails to do so and chase is given.

Chapter Twelve

PERSONAL INJURY

Introduction

Owners owe a duty to ensure the safety of persons on board the vessel. This duty extends beyond the physical limits of the vessel, where the safety of persons off the vessel is affected by the vessel's operation and the tasks carried out by the crew, eg. mooring operations, discharge with ship's crane. As regards the people whose safety is to be ensured, this is not limited to crew members, but extends to passengers, shore personnel and even unauthorised persons on board such as stowaways (see the section below on third party claims).

Personal injury is a massive source of claims for P&I Clubs, accounting for roughly 40% of all claims. If owners fail in their duty to ensure safety, the injured person will normally be entitled (depending on the jurisdiction), to compensation for suffering the injury, together with any loss of earnings, loss of pension rights or additional expenses, resulting from the accident.

In certain jurisdictions, in particular the USA, awards for personal injury are extremely high. It is important therefore that the Master and owners are vigilant in monitoring the safety of the vessel and working procedures. If they become aware of any potential risks to safety, action should be taken as soon as possible to remove the risk. The Master should also ensure that every incident which results in injury to crew or a third party, is recorded at the time, and the procedure detailed below follows.

This chapter examines the following:
Procedure in the event of an accident
Injury to crew
Injury to passengers, stevedores and other third parties
Evidence required from the vessel.

Procedure in the event of an accident

If a member of the crew is injured, the Master should ensure that a record of the accident is made as soon as practical. Most owners provide an accident form which should be completed in the event of an injury. An example of such a form for use in crew claims, is provided in Appendix 12:1.

If the injury is serious, the Master should telephone ashore for medical advise. In the event of a life threatening injury, if possible (depending on the vessel's position), the Master should consider medical help to be flown on board, or deviating to the nearest port. If time allows, owners should be informed of any deviation before it takes place and certainly afterwards. For less serious cases, medical assistance will be rendered on board by the crew unless the vessel is in port. The Master should ensure that a note is kept of the type of treatment administered to the injured person on board, any treatment administered to him ashore, by whom the treatment was administered, and the exact time the treatment was given. A record should also be kept of any medical advice sought.

The state authority (where the accident occurs), or flag state rules, may require details of the accident, eg. in the United Kingdom the Marine Accident Investigation Bureau form must be completed for "major" or "serious" injuries, in the following cases only:

i)   UK flagged vessels
ii) Any vessel in a UK port, and
iii) Passenger vessels carrying people to or from a UK port.

Further guidance should be sought from the Club/owners on reporting requirements.

After any injury owners/their insurers may request the attendance of lawyers and/or surveyors on board to interview the crew and inspect the scene of the accident. Even where this happens, it is still important for the Master, immediately after the accident, to collect the basic factual information, names of the witnesses, photographs and details of the scene of the accident, as it may be some time before the lawyers/surveyors are able to attend. In the event of death or very serious injury, the Master may find the local police or accident investigation body also attending to interview him and the crew. As with the accident report form, the Master should keep his answers as factual as possible and avoid speculating on the possible cause of the accident.

In the event that the injury was caused by a failure of a part of the ship's equipment, the Master should ensure that the damaged part is retained for future inspection. In certain jurisdictions, if owners are unable to produce the allegedly defective piece of equipment, there is a presumption that the equipment was damaged and owners will be put in a position of considerable disadvantage. If the item of ship's equipment is seriously damaged, the Master should request owners to call in a surveyor to inspect the damaged part.

Injury to crew

The owners' duty to ensure the crews' safety can be conveniently sub-divided into the following:

• To ensure a safe place of work

• To ensure the employment of competent crew

• To ensure the provision and maintenance of adequate appliances on board the vessel

• To ensure the provision of proper training, supervision and a safe system of carrying out the various tasks on board.

Owners' duty is effectively to carry out their operations without subjecting the crew to unnecessary risks to their safety. Where there is a foreseeable risk which owners could reasonably have taken steps to avoid, it will be considered an unnecessary risk. The risk to safety may be obvious, such as a faulty piece of machinery or oil spilt on the deck. It may, however, be less obvious, eg. young cadet inadequately trained.

Owners' duty extends beyond putting something right which is defective or broken, and may include improvements to working practices or the working environment which could reduce the risk of an accident. The following factors can be relevant, depending on the jurisdiction, in deciding whether there was a foreseeable risk:

• Whether there have been any similar accidents previously on this vessel or in the same fleet

• Whether the crew have previously reported a potentially dangerous situation

• Whether the safety committee on board have made any recommendations

• Whether there are any applicable safety guidelines, eg. published by the IMO or the flag state

• What the practices are in the industry

• Whether reports of similar accidents on board other vessels have been published.

It follows from the above that the Master and owners in trying to avoid accidents on board and personal injury claims, should be aware of any safety risks which these factors point to and take steps where possible to avoid those risks. The ISM Code requires a safety management system, which must include procedures to ensure that accidents and hazardous situations are reported to the company, investigated and analysed in order to improve safety (see section on the ISM Code in the introduction to this book).

Passengers

Owners' duty to ensure passenger safety, involves similar considerations to that of the crew, eg. a duty to maintain a safe living environment, and adequately trained crew and equipment (see crew section). Passenger injuries, especially on board cruise ships are fairly common, and care must be taken to ensure that as much factual detail as possible is recorded regarding the sequence of events when an accident occurs. An accident report form supplied by the owners should be completed by the Master or the Safety Officer. This should include the passenger's full name and address, as well as a space provided for the comments of the individual or any witnesses to the event.

In the case of a passenger reporting an injury to ship's personnel, his/her version of events should be recorded and their interpretation of how the accident was caused. At this point the Master should be careful not to concur with any statement provided or give his opinion on what has been said. Details of where the accident occurred on board should be included in the report being as precise as possible, and if deemed appropriate, photographs to be taken of the site and of any ship's equipment involved. Any medication or treatment administered to the passenger should be recorded, including when the medicine was given. Complaints of shipowners' negligence due to lack of medicine, professional assistance at the time of the illness/injury may be alleged at a later date.

Stevedores

The shipowner is obligated to provide a safe vessel and equipment at all times. Particular care should be given when a vessel enters a port/alongside as stevedores and other shore personnel will be boarding the vessel. Stevedore injuries may be caused due to their unfamiliarity with the ship's workings and fittings, therefore all crew should ensure that safe working procedures are followed strictly by the stevedores. During loading and discharge operations, the crew should ensure that all equipment, eg. ship's derricks, are used correctly. Also, that the deck is free of potential hazards, eg. loose electrical cables, oil.

Quite often the first evidence of an injury being sustained by a stevedore, will be several months or years later when a legal claim is presented to the owners. At that stage the owners will be in an extremely poor position to present the kind of evidence required or prepare a defence. Owners will be in a better position, if at least some details of the accident were recorded by the Master at the time.

In the event of a stevedore injury occurring, the procedures as described above for passenger injuries should be followed, the Master completing and accident report form at the first opportunity. If the injured stevedore does make any comments at the time about the accident or nature of the injury, these should be carefully recorded. It is of particular importance when a stevedore is injured that statements are taken from eye witnesses. This is because other stevedores who may have witnessed what happened, may not be contactable for their version of events in the future. Any statements should be attached to the accident report form, which makes it clear the information is confidential.

Other third parties

An owner is obligated to provide a safe environment for other persons on board the vessel, eg. crew relatives, stowaways. Again reporting procedures should be followed as soon as possible after injury occurring is known, with full personal and contact details of the injured party to be included. The third party's reason for being on board and exact time and place of the incident should also be included. In the case of stowaways, it is unlikely that injuries will be common place yet in such event it may be difficult to obtain details of the incident from the stowaway due to language barriers. However, a report prepared by the stowaway in his native language, if only to limit the extent of allegations, may assist in the event of a claim being presented.

If medical assistance is necessary, again all medication administered should be recorded in detail to avoid further allegation of negligence.

With any injury reported, the Master should try and avoid giving his opinion regarding the cause of the accident and confine himself to recording the facts of the investigation, to avoid implying shipowners' liability.

Evidence from vessel

- Investigating an accident

If the Master learns of an accident he should carry out the following investigations to try and establish as far as possible what happened. The investigation should be carried out as soon as practical after the accident

- **Examine the scene of the accident**. If possible, photographs should be taken, and signed on the reverse by the photographer with the time and date the photos were taken. Video film may also be extremely useful. It is also useful to have a note of the conditions where the accident occurred, eg. for a slipping injury, whether the deck was wet/dry, clean, unobstructed and whether it was daylight and what were the weather conditions - wind, sea state, rain, etc. If available use a lux meter to determine the lighting levels at the site of the accident. A sketch plan may also be useful

- **Check any relevant parts of the vessel's equipment or protective clothing to see if it was in good condition**. Any relevant piece of equipment must be retained. If for instance an accident occurs as a result of a broken wire or rope, samples should be kept for future analysis. Pieces of equipment or samples should, if possible, be placed in sealed bags, dated, signed for and witnessed. A note should be made as to whether the insured person was wearing any required safety equipment and wearing it correctly.

- **Interview the injured party, and any witnesses to the accident itself or to any relevant surrounding circumstances**. It is important for the person being interviewed to be at ease. Requests for information should be of a non-threatening nature. The injured person and/or witnesses may be defensive, feeling that the claim or allegation of fault could ultimately be directed against them. Advise the person you are interviewing that the purpose of the interview is to help determine the cause of the incident and to prevent further accidents of this type. If the injured person was not wearing the correct safety equipment then this should be recorded in the witness statement. A brief record of the interview should be kept and attached to the Master's report. In more serious cases where lawyers are attending, the Master should still investigate the accident, but leave written statements to them

- **The Master should always remember that he or his owners ought to contact the Club correspondents or the Club direct**, for advice on the investigation of any accident and the recording of evidence. Accidents which appear minor on the face of it, may lead to large claims depending on the jurisdiction. It is important to realise that it may be a year or two before a claim is made. Therefore it is crucial to obtain the evidence immediately after the accident and that this evidence is retained by the owner.

- Weight of evidence
  In the event the accident leads to a claim, some types of evidence carry more

weight than others, because their proximity to the accident makes them difficult to dispute. The most useful evidence will normally be from a witness who actually saw the accident, or from photographs showing the condition of the vessel or equipment. However, background evidence may also have its place. The following categories of evidence (strongest first), may assist:

- First hand evidence from eye witnesses who saw the accident happen

- Photographs, video evidence, pieces of equipment showing the scene of the accident and condition of equipment. It is important that these forms of evidence are taken as close in time to the accident as possible, and that nothing is moved or altered

- Witnesses who come on the scene shortly after the accident may also be valuable if they have additional information which backs up the eye witness, or in the event that no-one saw the accident happen

- Evidence as to the surrounding circumstances may also be important, eg. whether the injured party was drunk, what type of orders he had been given and whether he was supervised

- Speculation by witnesses as to the cause of an accident where this is not clear from the facts, may be prejudicial. A witness statement should record what was seen or heard. The witness should not give an opinion on the cause of the accident which he is not qualified to give. Equally, witnesses who just repeat what others have said happened (and not what they saw) is not useful. The exception being where the Master is unable to interview the source of the information, or the source of that information has changed his story.

- The master's report

The report should be headed as with the report form, "Confidential report prepared for the information of owners' solicitors and owners' P&I Club for use in litigation". Any basic report should include the following information in addition to a completed incident report form:

- **Details of the circumstances surrounding the incident**, eg. when and where the accident took place and the task which was being performed

- **The conditions at the time of the accident** and whether or not they contributed to the accident, eg. wet/dry, dark/light, deck clean, weather and sea state

- **Whether or not the injured party in any way contributed** to the accident and whether any third party was involved

- **The names and contact details of the witnesses to the accident**, including crew members and non-crew members. Briefly, what the witnesses saw and where they were positioned, unless the accident is serious and solicitors will be attending to take formal statements

- **What the injured party said happened at the time**, the nature of his injuries and whether he had any obvious pre-existing injury or bad health

- **Whether there was a system on board for carrying out the particular job** or any standing orders, and whether these were complied with. Whether there were any applicable safety procedures and whether these were complied with? Whether the work was supervised, if so, by whom?

- **Did the injured person comply with the requirements on the permit to work form**, eg. using a safety harness for working aloft

- **The report should as far as possible be a factual record** and not extend to guess work or personal opinions on what might have caused the problem. Remember all reports may be the subject of legal proceedings at a later date, often many years after a particular incident.

ACCIDENT REPORT DETAILS
CREW/PERSONAL INJURY
CONFIDENTIAL REPORT PREPARED FOR THE
INFORMATION OF OWNERS' SOLICITORS AND
OWNERS' P&I CLUB FOR USE IN ANY LITIGATION

(To be filled in by the Master in every case where an accident occurs)

1. Vessel..Type................................GRT......................

2. Owners' name and address..

3. Name of person injured ....

4. Seafarer, Stevedore, Shore Employee, please identify..

5. Address of person injured..

6. Date of Birth ....

7. Nationality..

8. Rating ....

9. Date of Accident............................Time............................Place......................

10. Date when injured crewman ceased work..

11. Port of Discharge............................Date..

12. Brief description of facts surrounding accident and nature of injuries showing
    how the injured person was employed at the time (attach copy of Log Entry
    and Report by Officer under whose supervision man was employed at the
    material time. If accident due to breakage of gear, broken parts must be
    carefully preserved) ....
    ....

13. Has the Reporting Officer visited the scene of the incident, if so at what time?
    ....

14. Date and time notice of accident received and by whom..

15. Particulars of medical treatment on board and/or given to whom given

....

16. State whether Doctor's Report submitted...

17. Has the injury incapacitated the seaman from work, totally or partially?

....

18. Was the injured person at his usual place of work when the accident

happened? If not, was he doing something he was authorised or permitted to

do for the purpose of his work? ....

....

19. Was he under the influence of alcohol or drugs?.....................................

20. Were any third party's involved in the incident? ....

If so, give name, address of employing company and occupation of same and

details of involvement..

....

21. Was the accident caused by collision? If so, give name and owners of colliding

vessel ....

....

22. What was the state of the light when and where the accident occurred? If

artificial lighting, give details ....

....

23. ANY FURTHER INFORMATION

Signed: Master ....Date:...

119

Chapter Thirteen

STOWAWAYS

Introduction

Historically, stowaways have caused considerable difficulties both to the Master and shipowner, particularly in areas of Africa and South and Central America where the problem is widespread. Additionally, there has been a significant rise in the number of cases where stowaways have boarded ships, seeking to flee countries which are in civil conflict, and also where it is the case that work is not available.

This chapter examines the following:

Procedures to prevent stowaways boarding a vessel

Procedures once stowaways have been discovered

Treatment of stowaways whilst on board

Diversion Expenses.

Procedures to prevent stowaways boarding a vessel

The Master should ensure that whilst the vessel is in port, a constant gangway watch is maintained. This may be done by utilising the services of crew, which although incurring the additional cost of overtime pay, will save the additional expense of instructing a private guard to carry out watch duty.

Prior to leaving the berth a thorough and systematic search of the entire ship should take place. This should include (depending upon the type of ship):

- The accommodation

- The engine room

- The decks (including the monkey island)

- The cargo compartments

- Unlocked store rooms

- Mast houses

- Enclosed spaces, eg forepeak, chain locker, steering gear compartment, etc.

- The lifeboats

- Any other spaces where people may hide.

Stowaway search checklists should be used wherever possible to confirm that each space has been searched, by whom and this should be dated and timed. An entry should be made in the log book confirming that the stowaway search was carried out and the results of the search.

Daily diligence will need to be taken in areas of the world where the problem of stowaways is most prevalent.

Procedures once stowaways have been discovered

If stowaways are discovered onboard the vessel, the Master should immediately inform the owner's agents at the next port of call, and owners who will generally inform their P&I Club, who will in turn, contact the local club correspondents for assistance. The stowaway(s) should be searched for any documentation (ie seaman's book, passport etc.) and a further search for any documents should be made on the vessel. Should any form of identity card be found, the repatriation process will be made much easier. If no documents are found, it is possible that the stowaways may be on board for a lengthy period of time whilst negotiations take place between the P&I correspondents, the local immigration authorities and the consul, or embassy of the alleged country of the stowaways.

If documents are not found, the stowaway should be questioned to try and discover relevant information.

A report with as much of the following information as possible should be sent as quickly as possible to the shipowners and/or the P&I Club, correspondents, agents:

• Last port visited

• Date and time of sailing from last port

• Does the vessel have cargo on board?

• How many stowaways have been found?

• When and where were the stowaways found?

• Do the stowaways have travel documents?

• Is communication possible with stowaways?

• State of health of stowaways

• Where have stowaways been placed?

• Do the stowaways pose any particular threat to the safety of the crew or vessel?

• Are the stowaways co-operative?

For each stowaway the following information should be provided (where possible):

• Full name

• Sex

• Date of birth

• Place of birth

- Name of both parents

- Home address

- Nationality.

Once this information is received then the shipowners, P&I Clubs, correspondents, etc. will liaise regarding further action to be taken regarding repatriation.

Once in port, the owner's agents, together with the P&I correspondents, will arrange for a full and formal interview and for photographs to be taken of the stowaways.

It is possible that stowaways will have to remain on board if there is either insufficient time to arrange for repatriation or if a local authority refuses to assist or to become involved.

Treatment of stowaways whilst onboard

Stowaways should be guarded as closely as possible, while the vessel is in port to prevent them from jumping ship and the owners therefore being held liable to pay heavy fines as a result of allowing "illegal immigrants" into a country. Moreover, if the stowaways are recaptured, owners will also be held liable for all future expenses inclusive of guard costs.

It is often the case that stowaways will be put to work onboard a vessel whilst a voyage is in process. Whilst this is an acceptable course of action to take, it is not one which would be recommended especially in cases where a significant number of stowaways are found onboard.

In cases as above, contact with the crew should be kept to a minimum as this may cause unrest. The stowaways should therefore be placed in secure quarters, guarded if possible and provided with adequate food and water to remain healthy.

- Records should be kept, and log entries made, of the following:

- What food, water and clothing provided to the stowaways

- Any medical treatment given to the stowaways

- Where the stowaways are being kept and the security arrangements in place

- Any additional security arrangements put in place, eg employment of shore security guards.

Diversion expenses

If it is decided to divert the vessel to land the stowaways, the shipowner may recover the expenses of doing so from his P&I Club. To do so, however, the owner will need to submit certain documentation from the vessel:

- Position of vessel when diversion commenced

- Date/time when diversion commenced

- Distance steamed and time taken to reach port of disembarkation of stowaways
- Details of fuel expenses
- Statement of facts
- Distance steamed and time taken to reach original course line
- Position, date and time diversion completed
- Details of fuel used during diversion
- Details of seamen's wages, stores and provisions used during the diversion.

It should be remembered however, that if the vessel has cargo on board then such a diversion would probably constitute a deviation. As such there would be a breach of the Contract of Carriage such that if the cargo was lost or damaged during the deviation, then the shipowner would not be in a position to rely upon the exceptions and defences of, for example, the Hague Rules. The shipowner would also prejudice his P&I cover.

Such a deviation should not therefore take place without clear instructions from the shipowners.

Chapter Fourteen

REFUGEES

Introduction

In certain parts of the world, the Master may encounter refugees in distress on the high seas. The United Nations High Commission for Refugees ("UNHCR") operates a scheme which is intended to minimise the problems faced by the Master and owners in the event refugees are taken on board the vessel to save their lives. Under this scheme, if the correct procedures are followed by the Master to record events and inform all the interested parties in good time, delay to the vessel may be avoided and compensation may be obtained to cover the expenditure stemming from the rescue of the refugees.

This chapter outlines the recommendations of the UNHCR contained in a booklet entitled "Guidelines for the disembarkation of Refugees".

In particular, this chapter examines the following:

Procedures in the event refugees are safely embarked on the vessel

Sequence of events

Owners' claims for compensation

Procedure

If the vessel on the high seas has taken on board refugees, the Master should immediately prepare a communication for owners and owners' agents at the next scheduled port containing the following information:

- Name of rescuing ship

- Flag and port of registry

- Name and address of managing owners

- Owners' agent at next scheduled port

- Estimated date and time of arrival at next scheduled port

- Estimated date and time of departure from next scheduled port

- Exact number of refugees on board

- Date, time, and exact location of rescue

- Details of events leading up to rescue

- State of health of refugees and details of any urgent medical assistance required

- A list of the refugees giving their full names, family groups, dates of birth, nationality and sex.

Sequence of events

Once the Master's message is received by the owners, the following sequence of events should begin and lead to the swift disembarkation of the refugees with the assistance of the UNHCR and the authorities involved:

- UNHCR and other authorities involved are informed of the refugee problem

- UNHCR and the flag state arrange for resettlement of the refugees

- Vessel arrives in the next scheduled port

- UNHCR issues guarantee of resettlement to local authorities

- UNHCR and local authorities board vessel to interview refugees

- Refugees disembark under care of UNHCR and cease to be the responsibility of the owners

- Refugees examined by local health authorities and await resettlement arrangements

- Finally, the UNHCR makes good the costs expended by the owners.

Claims for compensation

Once the refugees have disembarked from the vessel, the owners may submit their claim for compensation. The following items are recoverable from the UNHCR:

- Subsistence on board - US$10.00 per refugee per day

- Fuel used during any deviation to rescue refugees

- Communication expenses incurred as a result of the rescue

- Any additional port or agency charges incurred due to the presence of refugees on board

- Any loss of hire caused by delay in disembarkation.

At the time of publication of this book, the amount recoverable under any single claim cannot exceed US$30,000.00 except in exceptional circumstances.

The claim for compensation must be supported by as much documentation as possible. The Master will be required to provide statements giving details of time and fuel used during any deviation and provide copies of all messages sent and received. The Master also should make available a copy of the official log book entry covering the rescue. If possible, the Master should provide photographic evidence of the refugees.

It is important to note that the system of UNHCR assistance outlined in this section only applies to refugees arriving on board a rescuing ship at a scheduled port of call. Depending on the country involved, the system may not operate if a vessel deviates to a port for the specific purpose of disembarking refugees. Finally, the guidelines do not apply to refugees who directly enter into another country. As the worldwide refugee problem is continuously evolving, the Master should always verify the procedures outlined in this chapter with owners and their agents.

Appendix 14:1

REFUGEES

Case history

The vessel was on route from Miami to Nassau in the Bahamas. Approximately 20 miles west of Bimini three men were sighted on a raft. The chief mate reported the situation to the Captain. The Captain informed the mate to report the position of the raft to the US Coast Guard but not to stop and to continue to Nassau. The owners of the vessel were not advised of the situation.

Unfortunately, attempts to contact the US Coast Guard failed, although the chief mate alleged he had requested another vessel in the vicinity to inform the Coast Guard.

The raft contained refugees from Cuba who had been at sea for approximately five days. It was alleged after the vessel passed one of the rafters began drinking salt water. The refugees were rescued some twelve hours later when coast guards found them on Boyntun Beach. One of the refugees was hospitalised where he suffered from renal failure and septicaemia which necessitated the amputation of both legs and several other operations.

The injured refugee retained a lawyer in Miami who issued proceedings against the Master for an amount in excess of US$5 million. It was alleged that the Master had contravened at least two statues in not rendering assistance and this had led to the refugee ultimately suffering the aforementioned injuries.

The case proceeded to trial and the jury returned a verdict in favour of the Plaintiff in the gross amount of US$1,199,500.00. However, this was reduced to US$479,800.00 as the Plaintiff was found to be 60% comparatively negligent.

Comment

This case clearly illustrates the severe consequences that can arise if careful steps are not taken in dealing with refugee situations, particularly in the United States.

Although the case is an extreme one, it is also worthy of note that the proceedings themselves were successful against the Master.

THE NAUTICAL INSTITUTE

Shipping Management Series

The efficient operation of ships requires a high level of management skill. Shipping is a service industry and it is essential that it meets customer demands. Their requirements imply that the cargo will be loaded, carried and delivered in good order and condition and that the ship proceeds in a safe, timely and reliable way.

It is a fact that major disasters capture the headlines and influence public opinion, groundings, strandings, collisions, fires and explosions have become the driving force for new legislation and the focus of new safety training standards emanating from the IMO.

Some of the IMO training requirements are linked to safe ship operations like the new ISM Code and the courses on human resources under the STCW 95 Convention, but in general shipping management is excluded and the skills which go with it have to be provided by industry. To support industry in this endeavour the Council of The Nautical Institute has commissioned a series of training books and a video covering: ***Command; Watchkeeping Safety and Cargo Management in Port; Commercial Management for Shipmasters; The Management Diploma Scheme; Managing Safety and Quality in Shipping, a guide to ISM, ISO 9002 and TQM and The Mariner's Role in Collecting Evidence,*** Video and Book.

Command:– This is a major reference work covering all aspects of command at sea and is divided with six sections covering; Advice to new masters; Command law, commerce and training; Propulsion, control, communications, catering and maintenance; Navigation, seamanship and shiphandling; Case histories. It can be linked to a study programme for senior officers aspiring to command.

Watchkeeping Safety and Cargo Management in Port (Sponsored by the UK P&I Club) by Captain P. Roberts:- covers, Watchkeeping duties; Arrival; Mooring; Safety in Port; Taking over the watch; Commercial documentation; Break bulk cargo operations; Specialist dry bulk operations; Tanker operations; Ballast operations; Stress and stability; Cargo condition; Cargo quality; Ships Services; Pollution prevention; Ship's security; Securing the cargo; Keeping records; Departure and comprehensive appendices. The book is aimed at junior watchkeeping officers.

Commercial Management for Shipmasters (Sponsored by the UK P&I Club) by Mr R.L. Tallack:– covers, Contractual and management relationships between owner and master; Practical management techniques to be used on board; Budgets and management information systems; Terms of trade and bills of lading; Legal framework for contracts of carriage; Charter parties, the master's role as manager; Marine insurance; Contracts for purchasing supplies and services; Managing a technical cost centre; A changing approach to safety; Commercial perspectives on emprrnn li s renewal, sale purchase and financing supported by comprehensive appendices. The book is aimed at shipmasters and fleet managers.

The Management Diploma Scheme:– The Institute offers by distance learning, a series of modules aimed at improving personal effectiveness. The modules cover:– Setting objectives and planning; Controlling; Solving problems and making decisions; Leading and motivating staff; Delegating; Managing time; Running effective meetings; Coaching others.

Managing Safety and Quality in Shipping by Mr. A.M. Chauvel, covers, The evolution of safety management standards; Understanding the ISM Code; How to implement the ISM Code; ISM Certification; The ISO 9002 standard; Understanding the ISO 9002 standard; How to implement the quality standard; ISO 9002 certification; Towards total quality; Quality improvement management; Understanding the human element in quality improvement; Team work and organisation. The book is supported by helpful annexes.

The Mariner's Role in Collecting Evidence – Video. Linked to this book is an imaginative video, which can be obtained separately. It sets out to demonstrate that accident and loss prevention is an essential management discipline for controlling costs within the industry. The timely and accurate collection of evidence is the best defence that can be made against any claim and the video provides dramatic coverage to make this point with reference to cargo damage, pollution and personal injury.

The video can be bought separately from The Nautical Institute or hired as part of the Videotel Ship Hiring Service. If you want to hire the video please write or fax directly to:

Videotel Marine International
84 Newman Street
London W1P 3LD
Tel: 0171 299 1800
Fax: 0171 299 1818

For extra copies of The Mariner's Role in Collecting Evidence, purchase of the video and other books in the Management Series and The Nautical Institute's full publications list please write or fax to:

The Publications Officer
The Nautical Institute
202 Lambeth Road
London, SE1 7LQ
Tel: 0171 928 1351
Fax: 0171 401 2817